INSOLVENCY

Understanding the New Law

KPMG Peat Marwick McLintock

INSOLVENCY

Understanding the New Law

W.F. Ratford — R. Smith
of Peat Marwick McLintock

R.M. Gregory — M.J. Griffiths — J.S. Williams
of the Polytechnic, Wolverhampton

Financial Training

First published in Great Britain 1987 by Financial Training Publications Limited, Holland House, 140–144 Freston Road, London W10 6TR

Reprinted 1988

ISBN: 1 85185 062 7

Typeset by Kerrypress Limited, Luton
Printed by Livesey Limited, Shrewsbury

Contents

Acknowledgements

Whilst any errors in this book are the authors', we owe a debt to Richard Tapley for his advice and support and for his dedication in creating order out of chaos. We also thank Lyn Osborne, who efficiently converted manuscript to typescript and patiently accepted our never-ending amendments.

Abbreviations

The Act IA 1986	Insolvency Act 1986
The Rules IR 1986	The Insolvency Rules 1986 (S.I. 1986 No. 1925)
CDDA 1986	Company Directors Disqualification Act 1986
CA 1985	Companies Act 1985
CA 1976	Companies Act 1976
1914 Act	Bankruptcy Act 1914
I Reg	Insolvency Regulations 1986 (S.I. 1986 No. 1994)
IPR	Insolvency Practitioners Regulations 1986 (S.I. 1986 No. 1995)
S.I.	Statutory Instrument
S.I. 1986 No. 1996	Insolvency Proceedings (Monetary Limits) Order 1986
s.	section
r.	rule
reg.	regulation
sch.	schedule

Glossary of Insolvency Expressions

Administration order
A court order made in relation to a company in financial difficulties to allow the company to be rehabilitated or reorganised, or to ensure the most profitable realisation of the company's assets.

Administrative receiver
A receiver or manager of the whole or substantially the whole of a company's property appointed by (or on behalf of) the holders of any debenture of the company secured by a floating charge or by such a charge and one or more other securities.

Administrator
The person appointed under an administration order to manage a company to achieve the purpose set out in the order.

Bankrupt
A debtor (other than a corporate body) against whom a bankruptcy order has been made by the court; the order signifies that the debtor is unable to pay his debts and deprives the bankrupt of his property, which is then realised for distribution amongst his creditors.

Compulsory liquidation (winding-up)
Liquidation of a company ordered by the court as a result of a petition presented to it.

Creditors' committee
A committee formed to be representative of creditors as a whole to supervise the conduct of an administration or bankruptcy, or to receive reports from an administrative receiver.

Creditors' voluntary liquidation (winding-up)
Liquidation of a company, commenced by resolution of the shareholders but under the control of the creditors, which is unable to pay its debts in full within a period of twelve months.

Dissolution
The termination of the existence of a company, being effected by the registrar of companies at the conclusion of a liquidation.

Extortionate credit transaction
A transaction by which credit is provided upon exhorbitant or grossly unfair terms having regard to the risk accepted by the creditor, enabling the office holder to apply to the court for relief.

Fixed charge
A form of security, in favour of a creditor, over specific assets, preventing the debtor from dealing with those assets other than with the consent of the creditor.

Floating charge
A form of security granted by a company over its assets in favour of a creditor, in such manner that the company remains free to deal with those assets (the composition of which will change) in the ordinary course of its business as a going concern, unless and until an event occurs (a crystallising event) which causes the charge to become fixed in character thereby enabling the creditor to realise his security and recoup his debt.

Fraudulent trading
Trading with intent to defraud creditors of the company or any other creditor, or for any fraudulent purpose.

Insolvency practitioner
An individual authorised to act in insolvency matters either by a recognised professional body or by the 'relevant authority'.

Insolvency Practitioners Tribunal
An appeal authority to deal with cases where an individual has been refused an authorisation to act by the relevant authority or where an authorisation has been revoked.

Insolvency Rules
Delegated legislation made under the authority of the Insolvency Act 1986 to provide the detailed working procedures for the provisions of the Act.

Lien
A right of possession over goods or property belonging to another, with a right to retain possession until debts due to the possessor are

paid; also a form of equitable charge over property in favour of a creditor who may sell the property thus charged.

Liquidation
The process whereby a company ceases to trade and has its assets collected in and distributed to satisfy its liabilities; the term 'winding-up' is also used.

Liquidation committee
A committee formed to be representative of creditors as a whole to supervise the conduct of a compulsory or creditors' voluntary liquidation.

Liquidator
The name given to a person, other than the official receiver, who is responsible for dealing with the winding-up of the company; where the official receiver acts, he is known as 'the official receiver and liquidator'.

Members' voluntary liquidation
Liquidation of a company which is able to pay or provide for all its debts in full within a period of twelve months.

Nominee
The person named in a proposal to act in the preliminary stages of the implementation of a voluntary arrangement.

Office holder
A person who is acting as an insolvency practitioner in relation to a company.

Official receiver
A civil servant who deals with the administration of compulsory liquidations and bankruptcies.

Onerous property
Any unprofitable contract, or other property of an insolvent individual or company that is unsaleable or not easily saleable, or property that might give rise to some liability on the part of the company or trustee in bankruptcy.

Preferential debts
Debts that must be paid in priority to the holders of a floating charge

and in priority to unsecured creditors. These debts include PAYE, VAT and employees' remuneration.

Provisional liquidator
A person appointed by the court to protect the assets of a company after a winding-up petition has been presented but before the company is placed in liquidation.

Recognised professional bodies
Bodies recognised by the Secretary of State as incorporating in their rules appropriate provisions to ensure that those of their members that are authorised by them to act as insolvency practitioners are suitably qualified.

Receiver
The general term applied to the person administering any type of receivership.

Receivership
Where a lender holds a charge or mortgage over a company's assets as security for a debt, and in consequence of a default appoints a receiver to realise those assets to repay the debt.

Relevant authority
The authority appointed by the Secretary of State to deal with the authorisation of individuals to act as insolvency practitioners.

Shadow director
A person in accordance with whose directions or instructions the directors of a company are accustomed to act; however, he is not a shadow director merely because the directors act on advice given by him in a professional capacity.

Special manager
A person appointed by the court in a compulsory liquidation to assist the liquidator or provisional liquidator to manage the company's business.

Supervisor
A person appointed to supervise an approved voluntary arrangement.

Trustee in bankruptcy
The person who administers and realises the assets of a bankrupt,

and distributes the proceeds for the benefit of the bankrupt's creditors.

Unsecured creditor
A creditor who has a claim that will be paid out of realisations of a debtor's estate so far as there are assets to pay it. He has no special property rights as against the debtor (whether a company in liquidation or a bankrupt).

Voluntary arrangements
Compositions in satisfaction of debts and schemes of arrangement that are available in both corporate and individual insolvencies.

Voluntary liquidation (winding-up)
See creditors' voluntary liquidation and members' voluntary liquidation.

Winding-up petition
A petition presented to the court seeking an order of the court that a company be wound up (put into liquidation).

Wrongful trading
Where a director allows a company to continue trading in circumstances where he should have concluded that there was no reasonable prospect that the company would avoid going into insolvent liquidation; the director may be made liable to make a contribution to the company's assets.

Introduction

The process of reform of the structure of insolvency law in England and Wales has been completed by the consolidation of the Insolvency Act 1985 with the relevant parts of the Companies Act 1985 and the repeal of the Bankruptcy Act 1914. Thus, for the first time, all the principal provisions relating to the insolvency of companies and individuals are contained within one Act, the Insolvency Act 1986, other than those relating to company directors now found in the Company Directors Disqualification Act 1986.

Now that the new statutes have, for better or for worse, reached their final form, it is of interest to consider the long, and at times difficult, process that has resulted in a framework of insolvency law that is unlikely to change for many years.

Insolvency law in England and Wales, as it affects both bankrupt individuals and insolvent companies, has developed in a haphazard fashion over a long period of time, and is based upon statutes supplemented by the principles of common law and equity, all of which are in turn affected by case law. Much of the practice and principles of previous statutes were more suited to closing down the 'corner grocer's shop', selling the assets and distributing the proceeds to creditors, than to liquidating a substantial trading corporation with a multitude of assets, tangible and intangible, and with various groups of creditors with conflicting interests.

Against this background the Insolvency Law Review Committee was appointed in 1977, under the chairmanship of Sir Kenneth Cork, to carry out a fundamental and exhaustive review of the insolvency law in England and Wales. The final report of the committee was published in June 1982 (*Insolvency Law and Practice – Report of the Review Committee*, Cmnd 8558) and in addition to providing a comprehensive analysis of existing law and practice made proposals for new insolvency procedures and recommendations for the modernisation and improvement of existing procedures within the framework of a comprehensive and integrated insolvency system. The report also dealt with the qualifications and responsibilities of those administering insolvent estates, the treatment of assets and liabilities, and offences arising before and out of insolvencies.

In February 1984 the Government published its proposals for the reform of parts of insolvency law in the form of a White Paper (*A*

Revised Framework for Insolvency Law, Cmnd 9175). It is useful to quote from the introduction to the White Paper to illustrate the purpose of the proposals:

> The fundamental objectives of the Department of Trade and Industry are to encourage, assist and ensure the proper regulation of British trade, industry and commerce, and to promote a climate conducive to growth and the national production of wealth. In pursuing these objectives, the principal role of the insolvency legislation is:
>
> (i) to establish effective and straightforward procedures for dealing with and settling the affairs of corporate and personal insolvents in the interests of their creditors;
> (ii) to provide a statutory framework to encourage companies to pay careful attention to their financial circumstances so as to recognise difficulties at an early stage and before the interests of creditors are seriously prejudiced;
> (iii) to deter and penalise irresponsible behaviour and malpractice on the part of those who manage a company's affairs;
> (iv) to ensure that those who act in cases of insolvency are competent to do so and conduct themselves in a proper manner; and
> (v) to facilitate the reorganisation of companies in difficulties to minimise unnecessary loss to creditors and to the economy when insolvency occurs.

Whilst the aims thus expressed are admirable and were generally welcomed, the detailed proposals in the White Paper did not attract the same response and they met with considerable opposition. It is perhaps significant in the light of subsequent events that the timetable for introducing legislation was such that only six weeks were allowed for interested parties to comment on the proposals in the White Paper.

The Insolvency Bill was introduced in the House of Lords in December 1984, in the knowledge that a large number of amendments would be required to put the Bill into an acceptable form. In the event over 1,200 amendments were considered, many of them emanating from the Government, and the Bill had a controversial passage through both Houses of Parliament with the Government suffering two major defeats on its proposals. Furthermore, the reliance placed in the new law on delegated legislation was also, constitutionally speaking, somewhat controversial since the substance of some of the law, as opposed to merely its working procedures, was not known until the appropriate statutory instruments were published, and then only weeks before the Act came into force on 29 December 1986. As these procedures have been applied in practice, difficulties and anomalies have come to light. These Rules and Regulations made by way of statutory instruments are, even at this early stage, being reviewed. Some amendments will be made by the end of 1987 and it seems likely that other changes will be made, after due consideration, in 1988.

The new legislation does, however, have its good parts and one of the most valuable reforms is the creation of a profession of recognised qualified insolvency practitioners. In the long term this can only improve the standards of the administration of insolvents' estates and help to eliminate those whose activities were professional only in the sense that they were paid for.

The basic structure of corporate insolvency law set out in the Companies Act 1985 was unchanged, but two new procedures were added — a new company administration procedure designed to reorganise and revive companies that might otherwise go into liquidation (although experiments of this kind in America, Australia and South Africa have not been conspicuously successful) and voluntary arrangements (to which the Government was firmly committed in the White Paper).

The number of administration orders that have been granted by the courts has so far exceeded the expectations of those conversant with insolvency procedures, although it is too early to judge the benefits that will be achieved. There have also been amendments to liquidation procedures, and an attempt has been made to tighten control over delinquent directors and to tackle 'phoenix' companies.

The bankruptcy enactments represent a complete new code of law replacing the Bankruptcy Act 1914. The procedures leading to adjudication have been shortened and simplified; in particular, the acts of bankruptcy have been abolished, the doctrine of relation back has disappeared and the reputed ownership clause has been removed.

The law of fraudulent preferences for both liquidations and bankruptcy has been remodelled (though whether for the better is questionable). Also s. 172 of the Law of Property Act 1925 has been repealed and replaced with a new law on fraudulent conveyances in a way that is not an improvement upon the 1925 provisions, in that only transactions involving an undervalue are now impeachable.

A number of new expressions and concepts have been introduced and which are included in brief form in the glossary together with other terms in general use in connection with insolvencies.

Chapter 1

Insolvency Practitioners

1.1 Introduction

The Act introduces a system for authorising those engaged in insolvency work under which an individual is able to act as an insolvency practitioner only if he is authorised to do so by either: s. 390

(a) a recognised professional body; or
(b) the competent authority, being either the Secretary of State or a body set up by the Secretary of State for that purpose.

In addition an insolvency practitioner must provide security for the proper performance of his functions.

An insolvency practitioner must be an individual and is a person who acts in the following capacities:

(a) in relation to companies, as: s. 388

(i) liquidator;
(ii) administrator;
(iii) administrative receiver; or
(iv) supervisor of a voluntary arrangement under the Act;

(b) in relation to individuals or partnerships, as:

(i) trustee in bankruptcy, or interim receiver;
(ii) trustee under a deed of arrangement for the benefit of creditors;
(iii) supervisor of a voluntary arrangement under the Act;
(iv) administrator of an insolvent estate of a deceased individual; or
(v) in Scotland, permanent or interim trustee in a sequestration, or trustee under a trust deed for creditors.

s. 389 It is an offence to act as an insolvency practitioner whilst unqualified but the official receiver can act in any of these capacities without satisfying the above requirements.

1.2 Authorisation by recognised professional bodies

s. 391 A recognised professional body is one that incorporates in its rules appropriate provisions to ensure that those of its members who are authorised by it to act as insolvency practitioners are suitably qualified. The power to grant recognition lies with the Secretary of State, who may recognise any professional body that regulates the practice of its profession and maintains and enforces rules that ensure that any members who are permitted to act as insolvency practitioners are fit and proper persons and meet acceptable standards in education and in practical training and experience.

In the Insolvency Practitioners (Recognised Professional Bodies) Order 1986 recognition was granted to the Chartered Association of Certified Accountants, the Insolvency Practitioners Association, the Law Society, and the Law Society of Scotland, and the three Institutes of Chartered Accountants (England and Wales, Scotland and Ireland). Individuals who are not members of a recognised professional body but who are subject to its rules in the practice of their profession are, for the purposes of being qualified to act as insolvency practitioners, treated as being members of that professional body.

The recognition may be revoked if it appears to the Secretary of State that the body no longer satisfies the specified criteria but the effect of the revocation may be postponed for a specified period to allow the members of the body to continue to act for such period.

1.3 Authorisation by the competent authority

s. 392 An individual who cannot qualify as an insolvency practitioner through membership of a recognised professional body may apply for authorisation to act to the Secretary of State or to the competent authority appointed to deal with such matters by the Secretary of State. The application must contain the information required by the
s. 393 competent authority, and the authorisation will be granted if the competent authority is satisfied that the applicant is a fit and proper person to act as an insolvency practitioner and that he satisfies the prescribed educational and practical training and experience requirements. The authority also has the power to withdraw authorisation if the practitioner ceases to be a fit and proper person to act or if he fails to comply with the requirements of the Act, or if

the original authorisation was made on the basis of false, inaccurate or misleading information.

A refusal or withdrawal of authorisation must be notified, with reasons, to the individual involved, and there must be a statement of the individual's rights in the matter. He has 14 days from service of the notice to make written representations to the competent authority. If these are unsuccessful he may require the competent authority to refer his case to the Insolvency Practitioners Tribunal. He must do this within 28 days from service of the notice or, if he has made representations, within 28 days from notification that the competent authority does not intend to change its mind following his representations. Unless the competent authority has decided to grant, or not to withdraw, the authorisation and within seven days gives written notice of its decision to the applicant, it must refer the case to the tribunal for investigation and decision. The tribunal's report may be published if the competent authority thinks it fit to do so. If, within the period allowed, the applicant does not require the case to be referred to the tribunal, the competent authority may give him written confirmation of its refusal or withdrawal.

s. 394 s. 395 s. 396 s. 397 s. 398

1.4 Standards required for authorisation by the competent authority

The Insolvency Practitioners Regulations 1986 set out the criteria for judging whether an applicant to the competent authority is a fit and proper person to act as an insolvency practitioner and the educational standards he has to achieve. Factors which have to be taken into account in judging whether an applicant is a fit and proper person include:

IPR, reg. 4

(a) Whether he has been convicted of any offence involving fraud or other dishonesty or violence.

(b) Whether he has contravened any provision in any insolvency legislation, including any corresponding legislation in jurisdictions outside Great Britain.

(c) Whether, in the course of any business activities, he has engaged in practices which appear to be deceitful, oppressive or otherwise unfair or improper, or which cast doubt on his fitness to be authorised to act as an insolvency practitioner. These practices will be taken into account whether they are unlawful or not.

(d) Whether, in any previous insolvency practice he established and maintained adequate systems of control and adequate accounting and other records.

(e) If the applicant is already engaged in insolvency work, whether his practice is conducted with the necessary independence, integrity and professional skills appropriate to the range and scale of the practice and the performance of his duties. If the applicant is not already engaged in this type of work it has to be decided whether he will achieve these standards.

(f) Whether, if he has already acted as an insolvency practitioner, he has made full disclosure to interested parties of any actual or possible conflict between his duty and his own interests, whether financial, personal or otherwise.

IPR, reg. 4(2)

As well as being relevant to the decision whether or not to authorise a person to act as an insolvency practitioner, these criteria will also be applied where it is proposed to withdraw such authorisation on the grounds that the holder is not a fit and proper person.

IPR, reg. 5, sch. 1

An applicant who has not previously held an authorisation under the Act and who was not 35 years of age by 15 December 1986 must show that he has obtained the educational standard prescribed in the regulations or that he has achieved other academic or professional qualifications that are of an equivalent level.

There are also detailed provisions in the regulations to establish whether a person's practical training and experience are suitable.

IPR, reg. 8

Authorisation to act as an insolvency practitioner may be granted for a maximum period of three years.

1.5 Disqualification

s. 390

An individual will be disqualified from acting as an insolvency practitioner if:

(a) proper security, as required by the Act, is not in force (see 1.7 below);

(b) he is an undischarged bankrupt, or if sequestration of his estate has been awarded and he has not been discharged;

(c) he is subject to a disqualification order made under the Company Directors Disqualification Act 1986; or

(d) he is a patient within the meaning of Part VII of the Mental Health Act 1983 or s. 125(1) of the Mental Health (Scotland) Act 1984.

1.6 Insolvency practitioners' records

IPR, reg. 15, sch. 1

An insolvency practitioner appointed after 28 December 1986 to act in one of the capacities specified in s. 388 (set out above) must maintain a record of each insolvency proceeding in a specified form. On being given reasonable notice the practitioner must produce these records to the authorising body or its duly appointed representative. If the practitioner was authorised by virtue of his membership of a recognised professional body he must produce the records to the Secretary of State on being given reasonable notice. IPR, reg. 16

The practitioner must also notify the authorising body of the place where his records are kept and the place (if different) where, and the manner in which, they are to be produced. These records must be kept for a period of 10 years from the date on which the practitioner is granted his release or discharge in respect of the estate to which the records apply or from the date on which any security maintained in respect of that estate expired or otherwise ceased to have effect, whichever is the later. IPR, reg. 17

1.7 Security

Before an insolvency practitioner can act under an appointment made after 28 December 1986, he must satisfy the requirements for security in respect of losses caused by his fraud or dishonesty. IPR, reg. 10

The initial requirement is for a bond to provide general cover up to an amount of £250,000, which is lodged with the body from which the practitioner has obtained his authorisation. In addition, the bond must be extended in respect of each appointment taken by the practitioner by the issue of a certificate of specific penalty to provide cover for the assets involved in the particular proceedings. IPR, reg. 10

This certificate has to be obtained as soon as is reasonably possible after the practitioner's appointment and delivered within 14 days of receipt by the practitioner to the registrar of companies, the court or the accountant in bankruptcy in accordance with the regulations. IPR, regs 12, 13

The amount for which the certificate of specific penalty is issued is determined by the practitioner, based on any reports or statements of affairs available or his estimate of the assets involved. In the case of an administrative receiver the amount must be equal to the sum that would appear to be available to preferential and other unsecured creditors (thus excluding sums available only to secured creditors). Where a practitioner takes successive appointments in respect of an insolvency (for example, in a liquidation following an administration order) it is not necessary for him to obtain a new certificate. IPR, sch. 2

If at any time it appears to a practitioner that the value of assets is greater than originally estimated, a further certificate must be obtained but the value of the certificate cannot be reduced. In any case, the minimum sum for which a certificate of specific penalty can be obtained is £5,000 and if the value of the assets exceeds £5 million, the certificate is limited to that sum.

1.8 Insolvency Practitioners Tribunal

sch. 7 The Insolvency Practitioners Tribunal deals with cases where an individual has been refused an authorisation by the relevant authority, or where an authorisation has been revoked.

Membership of the Tribunal is drawn from two panels selected and from time to time revised by the Secretary of State. The first panel consists of persons who are barristers, advocates or solicitors each of whom must be of not less than seven years' standing and nominated for the purpose by the Lord Chancellor or the Lord President of the Court of Session. The second panel consists of persons who are experienced in insolvency matters. The Tribunal may sit either as a single tribunal or in two or more divisions and its functions must be exercised by a minimum of three members consisting of a chairman and two other members. The Secretary of State selects the chairman and the members.

The Tribunal is supervised by the Council on Tribunals and has the power to summon witnesses to attend and to produce such books and documentation as the Tribunal considers necessary to the investigation. It also has the power to take evidence on oath. Failure, without reasonable excuse, to answer a summons to attend, or intentional alteration, suppression, concealment or destruction of, or refusal to produce, any document required by the Tribunal is a criminal offence. The Secretary of State may make rules regulating the procedure in any investigation by the Tribunal.

1.9 Official receivers

ss. 399–401 The official receiver is any person authorised to act as such in relation to a bankruptcy or winding up. Official receivers are civil servants and are controlled by the Secretary of State. They are attached either to the High Court or to county courts with insolvency jurisdiction and are officers of the court.

Chapter 2

Voluntary Arrangements

2.1 Introduction

The Act contains procedures that provide a cheaper and less formal alternative to CA 1985, ss. 425 to 430, whereby a proposal may be made to a company and its creditors for a composition in satisfaction s. 1 of debts or a scheme of arrangement of the company's affairs. Under such a proposal, provision has to be made for an insolvency practitioner to act in relation to the composition or scheme, either as trustee or otherwise, for the purpose of supervising its implementation. This person is referred to as 'the nominee'.

The proposal can be made by the directors or by the liquidator if the company is in liquidation, or by the administrator if an administration order is in force. For the purpose of the proposal, the liquidator or administrator is known as 'the responsible insolvency practitioner' and may propose himself or another insolvency practitioner as the nominee. The purpose of the procedure is to enable a scheme or composition to be effected with the minimum involvement by the court.

2.2 The proposal

The proposal, whether made by the directors or by the liquidator or the administrator, must provide a short explanation of why it is believed that a voluntary arrangement is desirable and why the r. 1.3(2) company's creditors may be expected to agree with it. It must contain r. 1.3(1) details of the company's assets to be included in (or excluded from) the arrangement and assets to be provided by third parties, and the nature and amount of the company's liabilities. There must also be details of how the liabilities are proposed to be met, modified, postponed or otherwise dealt with under the arrangement, with particular reference to the claims of preferential, secured and connected creditors. The proposal must also state whether, to the proposer's knowledge, there are any circumstances which give rise to ss. 238 and 239 ss. 244 and 245 the possibility, in the event of the company going into liquidation, of any claims relating to transactions at an undervalue, preferences, extortionate credit transactions, or invalid floating charges, and, if there are, what provision has been made to indemnify the company in respect of such claims.

r. 1.3(2) Other information to be given in the proposal includes the nature of any guarantees of the company's debts given by other persons and the relationship of the guarantors with the company; the proposed duration of the voluntary arrangement and the proposed dates of distributions to the creditors, with estimates of the amounts; the amount to be paid to the nominee and supervisor of the arrangement by way of remuneration and expenses; details of the supervisor's functions and his qualifications; whether the directors or others are offering guarantees for the purposes of the arrangement and, if so, whether any security is to be given or sought; the way in which funds held for the purpose of the arrangement are to be managed pending distribution; what is to be done with undistributed funds once the arrangement has ended; the way in which the company's business is to be conducted during the course of the arrangement; and finally, details of any credit facilities that are to be arranged for the company and the way in which the debts arising thereunder are to be dealt with.

2.2.1 Proposal where liquidator or administrator is not the nominee

r. 1.12 Where the proposal is made by the liquidator or administrator and names another insolvency practitioner as the nominee, or where it is r. 1.4 made by the directors of the company, the intended nominee must be given notice of the proposal. If the intended nominee agrees to act, he r. 1.12 must have a copy of the notice endorsed with the date of receipt and he must return this copy to the person who made the proposal.

r. 1.5 Within seven days of delivering the proposal to the nominee, the directors, or the responsible insolvency practitioner, must deliver to the nominee a statement of the company's affairs, although this period may be extended by the nominee. The statement must include r. 1.5(2) details of the company's assets with values, details of the company's creditors and shareholders, and particulars of any debts owed to or r. 1.6 by persons connected with the company. (A person is connected with a company if he is a director or shadow director of the company or his associate.) The nominee may also request any other information to enable him to prepare a report on the proposal. Amongst other things, the nominee may require details about any person who is, or at any time during the preceding two years was, a director of the company and whether in that period that person has been concerned in the affairs of any other company that has become insolvent or

whether he has been adjudged bankrupt or has entered into an
arrangement with his creditors. The nominee must also be given s. 249
access to the company's accounts and records in order to help him to
consider the proposal.

Within 28 days of receiving the proposal, the nominee must submit r. 1.7
to the court a report, based on the proposal, stating whether, in his s. 2
opinion, meetings of the company and its creditors should be
summoned to consider the proposals and, if appropriate, the date,
time and place that he proposes for the meetings. He must also
deliver to the court a copy of the proposal and a copy or summary of
the company's statement of affairs and he must send a copy of the
report and his comments to the company.

If the nominee fails to submit a report the court may, on s. 2(4)
application by the person intending to make the proposal, order that
the nominee be replaced by another insolvency practitioner. The r. 1.8
original nominee must be given at least seven days' notice of this
application.

If the nominee concludes in his report that meetings of the r. 1.9
company and its creditors should be summoned to consider the proposals and the court does not direct otherwise, he must fix a date for such meetings to be held within 14 to 28 days of the filing of his report in the court. The nominee must give at least 14 days' notice of the meeting specifying the court to which his report has been delivered and the notice of the meeting must be accompanied by a copy of the proposal, a copy or (if the nominee thinks fit) a summary of the statement of affairs, including a list of creditors and the nominee's comments on the proposal. If the nominee is calling a creditors' meeting, he must notify all the creditors specified in the statement of affairs and any other creditors of the company of whom he is aware. If a meeting of members of the company is being called, notice must be given to all persons who are, to the best of the
nominee's belief, members of it. At least 14 days' notice of the r. 1.16
meeting must also be given to all directors of the company and to all those whose attendance the person calling the meeting considers relevant, including officers of the company and anyone who has been a director or officer of it in the preceding two years.

2.2.2 Proposal where liquidator or administrator is the nominee

If the proposal is made by the liquidator or administrator acting as nominee, the proposal must contain all the information outlined above, together with any further matters that the responsible insolvency practitioner considers appropriate to enable members and creditors of the company to make an informed decision on the proposal. The nominee is not required to submit a report to the court

r. 1.9 but he must call a meeting of the creditors and of the members of the company, giving at least 14 days' notice. The notice must be accompanied by a copy of both the proposal and the statement of affairs although, if he thinks fit, the nominee may send a summary of the statement, including in the summary details of all creditors.

If the company is being wound up by the court, notice of the proposal must be given by the responsible insolvency practitioner to the official receiver. If someone other than the responsible insolvency practitioner is to act as nominee, the notice must be accompanied by the name and address of that person.

2.3 The meetings

The purpose of the creditors' and company meetings is to decide
r. 1.13 whether to approve the proposals. Proxy forms and a summary of the rules relating to majorities at creditors' meetings must be sent out with every notice of meeting. The meetings must be held on the same day and in the same place between 10 a.m. and 4 p.m. on a business day and the venue must be fixed primarily to suit the convenience of the creditors, whose meeting must be held before that of the
r. 1.14 company. The meetings will be chaired by the convenor or by a nominated substitute, who must be either a qualified insolvency practitioner or an employee of the convenor, or of the convenor's firm, who is experienced in insolvency matters. The chairman has the
r. 1.16(2) power to exclude any present or former director or officer from the meeting or any part of it, and to admit or reject all or any part of a creditor's claim for the purpose of his entitlement to vote. A
s. 4.6 report of the meeting must be made by the chairman to the court and,
r. 1.17(8) within 28 days of this report, the chairman's decision whether to
r. 1.17(5) accept or reject a claim may be appealed against by any creditor or
r. 1.17(7) member. If the court considers that what has happened gives rise to unfair prejudice or material irregularity it may order another meeting to be summoned or make such other order as it thinks fit. If
r. 1.17(6) the chairman is unsure whether to admit or reject a claim, he must mark it as objected to and allow the creditor to vote. Should the objection to the claim later be upheld, the creditor's vote will be declared invalid.

r. 1.17(1) Every creditor who has been given notice of the creditors' meeting
r. 1.19(3) is entitled to vote at the meeting or any adjournment of it. If a creditor fails to give the chairman written notice of his claim either before or at the meeting, however, his vote will not be counted. The
r. 1.17(2) vote will be calculated according to the amount of the creditor's debt
r. 1.17(3) although there is no voting right for unliquidated debts or for those whose value is unascertained unless the chairman estimates a

minimum value for them. r. 1.19(3) The votes of secured creditors will not be counted except, presumably, for the unsecured part of their claim for which the chairman has received written notice before or at the meeting. In these circumstances the chairman may exercise his discretion and allow the vote to count.

r. 1.19(1) At the creditors' meeting a resolution to approve the proposal or any modification must be passed by a majority of three-quarters in value of creditors present, in person or by proxy, and voting. r. 1.19(2) Other resolutions must be passed by a simple majority. r. 1.19(4) A resolution, however, will be invalid if those who vote against it include over half in value of the 'creditors'. For this purpose, 'creditors' includes those to whom notice of the meeting was sent, whose votes have not been excluded by the chairman in accordance with r. 1.19(3) and who the chairman believes are not persons connected with the company.

r. 1.18(1) Company members may vote according to the rights attached to their shares or other interest in accordance with the articles of association. r. 1.18(2) Even if no voting rights attach to a member's shares, he may vote for or against the proposal or any modification of it. However, the rules do not clarify how such votes are to be valued.

r. 1.20 At the meeting of the company a simple majority of those present in person or by proxy and voting will, subject to any express provision in the company's articles, be sufficient to pass a resolution although a vote by members whose shares do not carry any voting rights will not count towards the majority.

r. 1.15 The chairman may hold a proxy vote but, unless otherwise directed by the proxy, he may not use this vote to vary the remuneration or expenses of the nominee or supervisor of the arrangement. r. 1.19(6) If he does so, his vote with the proxy will not count towards any majority at either the creditors' or the company meeting.

r. 1.21 The rules provide that the meetings may be adjourned or combined until the proposal is either accepted or rejected by creditors and members. If, on the day on which they were summoned, the meetings do not approve the proposals, the chairman may adjourn both meetings for up to 14 days. If the meetings were called to consider a proposal from the company's directors, the nominee must give notice of the adjournment to the court. r. 1.21(6) If, following any final adjournment of the meetings, the proposal is not agreed by both meetings it is deemed to be rejected.

s. 4 The meetings may give approval to a proposal either with or without modifications. If approval is given subject to the scheme or composition being modified, however, such modification must not alter the proposal in such a way that it is taken outside the definition of a voluntary arrangement. Futhermore, the meetings cannot approve any proposal or modification that affects the rights of any secured or preferential creditor to be paid in priority or the right of preferential creditors to be paid *pari passu* with each other, unless those creditors concur. The term 'preferential debt' is given the same meaning as in the context of a liquidation, and the relevant date for determining such debts where the company is not in liquidation is the date of the making of the administration order, if one has been made, or the date of the approval of the proposal in other cases.

s. 4(6)
r. 1.24
The chairman must prepare a report on the result of the meetings and, within four days of the meetings, file a copy of this with the court. At the same time he must give notice of the results to all those who were sent notice of the meetings. The report must state whether or not the proposal was accepted and any modifications that were made; what resolutions were taken and the decisions made on each; which creditors and members (with their respective values) were at the meetings, whether in person or by proxy, and how they voted on each resolution; and any further information that the chairman thinks appropriate. If the meetings approve the proposal, a copy of the chairman's report must be sent to the registrar of companies.

s. 5
If the proposal is approved, the composition or scheme will take effect as if it had been made by the company at the creditors' meeting. Thereafter, every person who had notice of and was entitled to vote at the meeting, whether or not they actually did so, is bound by the proposal. If approval is given to a proposal and, at the time, the company is being liquidated or is subject to an administration order, the court may stay all proceedings in the liquidation, or discharge the administration order or give directions as it thinks fit to facilitate the implementation of the composition or scheme. However, the court may not make an order staying liquidation proceedings or discharging the administration order before the end of a 28-day period beginning with the first day on which each of the reports on the results of the meetings has been made to the court, or at any time when an application to challenge the decision or an appeal in respect of such an application is pending, or at any time in the period within which such an appeal may be brought.

2.4 Challenge of decisions

s. 6
Within 28 days of the reports of the meetings being made to the court an application challenging the meetings' decisions may be made either:

(a) by a person entitled to vote at either of the meetings;
(b) by the nominee or any person who has replaced him; or

(c) if the company is being wound up or is subject to an administration order, by the liquidator or administrator.

The challenge may be made on the grounds that the composition or scheme approved at the meetings unfairly prejudices the interests of a creditor, member or contributory of the company and/or that there had been some material irregularity at or in relation to either of the meetings. It should be noted that apart from these provisions, an approval given at a meeting shall not be invalidated by any irregularity at or in relation to the meeting.

The person making the application must serve sealed copies of it on the supervisor of the arrangement and on the directors or administrator or liquidator (according to who made the proposal for the arrangement). r. 1.25(2)

If the court is satisfied that there is a valid ground for challenging the meetings' decisions it may revoke or suspend the approvals given by the meetings; also, or in the alternative, the court may give a direction to any person for the summoning of further meetings to consider any revised proposal that the original proposer may make.

If the court orders that further meetings be summoned, notice must be given to the person who is, according to the court's direction, required to summon the meetings. The directors, liquidator or administrator (whichever is the appropriate person) must thereupon give notice of the court's order to all persons who were sent notice of the meetings and to all others who appear to be affected by the order and, within seven days of receiving a copy of the court order, must inform the court whether it is intended to make a revised proposal to the company and its creditors, or to invite reconsideration of the original proposal. A copy of the court's order must, within seven days of its being made, be sent to the registrar of companies by the person on whose application the order of revocation or suspension was made. r. 1.25(3) r. 1.25(4) r. 1.25(5)

If, after the court has directed that meetings should be summoned to consider revised proposals, it transpires that the person who made the original proposal does not intend to submit a revised proposal, the court must revoke the direction and revoke or suspend any approval given at the previous meetings. If the challenge is based on a material irregularity in relation to either of the meetings, the court may revoke or suspend the approval given by the meeting in question, and may give a direction that the meeting be reconvened to reconsider the original proposal.

In giving directions, or in revoking or suspending an approval, the court may give such supplemental directions as it thinks fit. In particular it may give directions with respect to things done since the meeting under any composition or scheme approved by the meeting.

2.5 The supervisor

s. 7 If a proposal is approved and is not subject to a challenge, the person who is carrying out the functions of the nominee becomes known as
r. 1.22(3) the supervisor of the composition or scheme. If at either meeting it is resolved that a person other than the nominee be supervisor of the arrangement, that person must give the chairman, in writing, his consent to act, and confirmation that he is qualified to act as an insolvency practitioner in relation to the company. The supervisor must be put in possession of the assets included in the arrangement
r. 1.23(2) and, once he is in possession, he must discharge any balance due to the responsible insolvency practitioner by way of remuneration or on account of any properly incurred fees, costs, charges and expenses and any advances made in respect of the company plus interest from the date the company went into liquidation or, as the case may be, became subject to the administration order. As an alternative to immediate payment, the supervisor may give the responsible insolvency practitioner a written undertaking to discharge any balance outstanding out of the first realisation of assets. Until he receives payment, the responsible insolvency practitioner has a charge on the assets covered by the arrangement, and all guarantees he has properly given for the benefit of the company must be discharged out of the assets. In this context, the phrase 'responsible insolvency practitioner' includes, where the company is being wound up by the court, the official receiver, whose claims take priority over those of the liquidator.

The supervisor acts under the supervision of the court and may apply to the court for directions in relation to any particular matter arising under the composition or scheme. He is one of the persons who may apply to the court to have the company wound up or to have it made subject to an administration order. Should any of the company's creditors or any other person be dissatisfied by any act, omission or decision of the supervisor he may apply to the court, which has the power to confirm, reverse or modify any such act or decision. It may also give the supervisor directions or make such other order as it thinks fit.

In cases where it is both expedient to appoint a person to carry out the functions of the supervisor and inexpedient, difficult or impracticable for such an appointment to be made without the court's assistance, the court may make an order to fill a vacancy, or to increase the number of supervisors, replace a sole supervisor or replace one or more supervisors where there is more than one acting.

During the course of the voluntary arrangement the supervisor is required to keep accounts and records of his transactions and, in particular, records of all receipts and payments of money. At a maximum of 12-monthly intervals, the supervisor must prepare an abstract of receipts and payments and, within two months, send a copy to the court, the registrar of companies, the company, those creditors bound by the arrangement, those members of the company who are also bound (the court may dispense with this requirement), and, if the company is not in liquidation, the company's auditors for the time being. Along with the abstract, he must also send comments on the progress and efficacy of the arrangement. The Secretary of State may, at any time during the course of the arrangement or after its completion, require the supervisor to produce for inspection his records and accounts, and copies of the abstracts and reports he has prepared. The Secretary of State may order that the accounts and records be audited, and that the supervisor gives such further information and assistance as is necessary for this purpose. r. 1.26(2) r. 1.27

Hitherto, certain monopoly suppliers of utility services have been able to insist on the payment of outstanding accounts due by the company before they would allow a supply to the office holder. This is now illegal under the Act but the supplier is entitled to require a personal guarantee from the supervisor in respect of future supplies. The services covered by this provision are: s. 233

(a) a public supply of gas;
(b) a supply of electricity by an electricity board;
(c) a supply of water by statutory water undertakers;
(d) a supply of telecommunication services by a public telecommunications operator.

After the arrangement has been completed, the supervisor must, within 28 days, send to all creditors and members of the company who were bound by the arrangement and to the court and the registrar of companies, notice that the arrangement has been fully implemented in accordance with the proposals. This notice must be accompanied by a report summarising all receipts and payments made by the supervisor and giving an explanation of any difference in the actual implementation of the proposal as compared with the proposal as approved by the creditors' and company meetings. r. 1.29

Chapter 3

Administration Orders

3.1 Introduction

The Act introduced a new procedure whereby the court is empowered to make an 'administration order' in regard to a company in financial difficulties with the effect that the management of the company is placed in the hands of an administrator and that, for the period during which the order is in force, the company cannot be wound up nor can any proceedings or process, charge, hire-purchase or other specified agreement be enforced against the company without leave of the court.

Before making an administration order the court must be satisfied
s. 123 that the company is, or is likely to become, unable to pay its debts
s. 8 and it must consider that the making of an order would be likely to achieve one or more of the following purposes:

s. 8(3) (a) the survival of the company, and the whole or any part of its undertaking as a going concern;

(b) the approval at a meeting of the company and its creditors of a composition in satisfaction of the company's debts or a scheme of arrangement of its affairs;

(c) the sanctioning under CA 1985, s. 425, of a compromise or arrangement;

(d) a more advantageous realisation of the company's assets than would be effected on a winding up.

3.2 Application for an administration order

s. 9 Application is by petition to the court, presented by the company, the directors, a creditor or creditors (including any contingent or prospective creditor or creditors) or any combination of these. A
r. 2.3 representative of the applicant must swear an affidavit stating the deponent's belief that the company is, or is likely to become, unable

to pay its debts and the grounds for that belief, and which of the purposes in s. 8(3) above is expected to be achieved by the making of the administration order. There must also be provided a statement of the company's financial position, listing its assets and liabilities (including liabilities that are contingent and prospective) and detailing any security held by creditors and whether the security gives the power to appoint an administrative receiver. If an administrative receiver has been appointed, this must be stated. Details of any winding-up petition must be included in the affidavit as must any other matters the petitioner considers will help the court decide whether to make an administration order.

The petition may be supported by the report of an independent person, either the proposed administrator or someone who has adequate knowledge of the company's affairs. The report should specify which purpose in s. 8(3) above might be achieved by an administration order and should state that the appointment of an administrator for the company is expedient. Although, unlike the affidavit, the report is not a prerequisite for the hearing of a petition, an explanation must be given if one is not submitted. r. 2.2

The petition must give the name and address of the proposed administrator, and must be accompanied by a statement that he is a qualified insolvency practitioner and a written consent by him to accept appointment if an administration order is made. The petition and affidavit will be filed in court, and the court will then fix a hearing. Copies of the petition, the affidavit and its exhibits must be served on any person who has appointed, or has the power to appoint, an administrative receiver for the company; on an administrative receiver, if one has been appointed; on any petitioning creditor if a petition for the liquidation of the company is pending; on the petitioner and on the provisional liquidator, if any; and on the proposed administrator. If the petition for the administration order is presented by creditors of the company the petition must be served on the company. The copies of the petition must be served not later than five days before the date fixed for the hearing, and service must be verified by an affidavit to be filed in court no later than the day before the hearing of the petition. Once a petition has been presented it cannot be withdrawn without leave of the court. r. 2.4 r. 2.5 r. 2.6 r. 2.7 r. 2.8

At the hearing, those entitled to appear or to be represented are the petitioner, the company, any person who has appointed or is entitled to appoint an administrative receiver, the administrative receiver if already appointed, the proposed administrator, any person who has presented a petition for the liquidation of the company, and, with the leave of the court, any other person who appears to have an interest.

3.3 Effect of an application

s. 10 While the court is considering whether to grant or refuse an order no resolution may be passed or order made for the winding up of the company. Furthermore, the court's consent must be obtained before any action is taken to enforce any security over the company's property (other than the appointment of an administrative receiver) or to repossess goods in the company's possession under any hire-purchase, chattel leasing, retention of title or conditional sale agreement and before any other proceedings, execution or other legal process, including the levying of distress, is commenced or continued against the company or its property. If the court grants leave, it may do so subject to any terms it sees fit to impose.

The period during which these restrictions operate may be varied if, at the time the petition is presented, the company is in the hands of an administrative receiver and the person by or on whose behalf he was appointed has not consented to the making of the administration order. In this event, the period during which the restrictions operate will be deemed not to begin until that person so consents.

Leave of the court does not have to be sought for the presentation of a petition for the winding up of the company, nor for the appointment of an administrative receiver to the company nor for the carrying out by such a receiver, whenever he is appointed, of his functions.

3.4 Powers of the court

s. 9 On hearing a petition, the court has the power to dismiss it, or to adjourn the hearing conditionally or unconditionally, or to make an interim order or any other order that it thinks fit. An interim order may restrict the exercise of any powers of the directors or of the company by, for example, requiring that, before action is taken, the consent of the court or of a person qualified to act as an insolvency practitioner in relation to the company is obtained.

Where the court is satisfied that there is an administrative receiver of the company, it has to dismiss the petition unless:

(a) the person by whom, or on whose behalf, the administrative receiver was appointed has consented to the making of the order, thereby agreeing to the termination of the receivership; or

(b) the court is satisfied that, were an administration order to be made, any security by virtue of which the administrative receiver was appointed would be liable to be released, discharged or avoided (under the provisions relating to transactions at an undervalue, preferences and the avoidance of certain floating charges) or be subject to challenge under CA 1985 or under any rule of law in Scotland.

Thus, a floating-charge holder whose security is not liable to be set aside and who has not yet appointed an administrative receiver may prevent an administration order being made against the company by appointing such a receiver before the court reaches its decision on the petition. Furthermore, an administration order cannot be made s. 8
where a company has gone into liquidation, or where it is an insurance company, a recognised bank, a licensed institution within the meaning of the Banking Act 1979 or one which is treated as being so licensed. Subject to these limitations, the court may make an administration order where the conditions set out in 3.1 are satisfied, and the court order must specify the purpose or purposes for which the order was made.

3.5 Notification of appointment

Once the court has made the order it must forthwith give notice to the s. 21
person appointed as administrator and he must advertise it once in r. 2.10
the *Gazette* and once in such newspaper as he thinks most appropriate for ensuring that it comes to the notice of the company's creditors. He must also give notice of the administration order to the company. Within 14 days of the making of the order, the administrator must send a copy of it to any person who has r. 2.10(3)
appointed an administrative receiver or has the power to do so, to any administrative receiver, to any petitioner for the winding up of the company, to any provisional liquidator, and to the registrar of companies. Within 28 days, unless the court otherwise directs, the administrator must also send notice to all the creditors of the company in so far as he is aware of their addresses.

Failure without reasonable excuse to comply with these requirements renders the administrator liable to prosecution.

3.6 Effect of the administration order

The administration order will direct that, during the period for which it remains in force, the affairs, business and property of the company shall be managed by the administrator appointed for the purpose by the court. Once the order is made, any petition for the liquidation of s. 11(1)
the company is dismissed and if a receiver of only part of the company's property has been appointed, he must also vacate office if s. 11(2)
required to do so by the administrator. If an administrative receiver s. 11(1)

is in office he must vacate that office, but his remuneration and
s. 11(4) expenses properly incurred and any indemnity to which he is entitled out of assets will constitute a charge on the property of the company that is in his custody or under his control at that time, and will rank in priority to any security held by the person by or on whose behalf he
s. 11(5) was appointed. Any receiver who vacates office following and because of the granting of an administration order is relieved of the duty under s. 40 or s. 59 to pay preferential creditors.

s. 11(3) While an administration order is in force there can be no resolution passed or order made for the liquidation of the company nor may an administrative receiver of the company be appointed. Further, unless the administrator gives his consent or the court gives leave (subject to such terms as it thinks fit), no steps may be taken to enforce any security over the company's property or to repossess goods in the company's possession under any hire-purchase, chattel leasing, retention of title agreement or conditional sale agreement. Unless consent or leave of the court is obtained, no other proceedings, execution or other legal process may be commenced or continued and no distress may be levied against the company or its property.

s. 12 While an administration order is in force, the fact that the company is being managed by an administrator, together with the name of the administrator concerned, must be stated on all documents issued by or on behalf of the company or the administrator. Failure to do this will render the company, and the administrator or any officer of the company, if without reasonable excuse they authorised or permitted the default, liable to prosecution.

3.7 Administrators

s. 13 An administrator may be appointed either by an administration order or by an order of the court made to fill a vacancy in the office of administrator caused by death, resignation or other event. In the latter cases, an order may be made on the application of any continuing administrator of the company or, if there is no such administrator, by the creditors' committee (see 3.8.5 below) or, failing either of these, by the company, the directors or any creditor or creditors of the company.

r. 2.47 The administrator will be paid an amount fixed either as a percentage of the property with which he has to deal or by reference to the time properly spent by him and his staff in dealing with the administration. The creditors' committee will decide which method is to be employed, taking into account such factors as the complexity of the case; whether the administrator had to undertake exceptional responsibility; how effectively the administrator performed his duties; and the value and nature of the property being dealt with. In the absence of a creditors' committee, or if the committee does not make a decision, the administrator's remuneration may be fixed by a resolution at the creditors' meeting or by the court.

If the administrator is dissatisfied with the rate or the amount of the remuneration fixed by the creditors' committee he may request its increase by resolution of the creditors or, failing that, by order of the court. He must give at least 14 days' notice of his application to the court to the creditors' committee which may nominate one or more of its number to be heard on the application. In the absence of a committee, notice must be sent to such one or more of the creditors as the court may direct and they may nominate one of their number to appear or be represented at the hearing. r. 2.48 r. 2.49

If 25% in value of the creditors consider that, in all the circumstances, the administrator's remuneration is excessive, one of their number may apply to the court to have the amount reduced. The court may dismiss the application subject to the applicant being given at least seven days' notice of an *ex parte* hearing that he may attend. If the court decides to hear the application, the applicant must give the administrator at least 14 days' notice of the hearing and provide him with a copy of the application and of any evidence being adduced in support of it. The court has the power to reduce the rate or amount of the administrator's remuneration if it considers the applicant's claim proved. r. 2.50

3.8 Duties of an administrator

The major function of an administrator is the preparation and proposal of a plan to achieve, or attempt to achieve, the purpose or purposes specified in the administration order. Such a plan may be for the rehabilitation or reorganisation of the company or for the most profitable realisation of the company's assets for the benefit of its creditors and members. He has three months in which to prepare the plan, unless the court extends this period, and by the end of that time he must put his proposal to the creditors of the company. The proposals may be accepted, modified or rejected by the creditors, and the details and ramifications of this are dealt with in 3.8.2 and 3.10 below.

In the period before the proposals receive approval the administrator will manage the affairs, business and property of the company in accordance with any directions given by the court. If and when the proposals are approved, he will manage the affairs, s. 17(2) business and property of the company in accordance with those proposals, and in accordance with any subsequent revisions to those proposals.

3.8.1 Statement of affairs

s. 22 The administrator shall forthwith on appointment require the preparation and submission to him of a statement of the affairs of the company from some or all of the following:

(a) those who are or have been officers of the company;

(b) those who have taken part in the company's formation at any time within one year before the date of the administration order;

(c) those who are in the company's employment or have been in its employment within that year, and are, in the administrator's opinion, capable of giving the information required;

(d) those who are, or have been within that year, officers of or in the employment of a company that is, or within that year was, an officer of the company. In this context 'employment' includes employment under a contract for services.

r. 2.11 The administrator must send notice of his requirement to the relevant persons specifying: the names and addresses of all others to whom the same notice has been sent, the time within which the statement must be delivered (within 21 days beginning with the day after that on which notice is given), the penalties for non-compliance, and the general duty of officers under s. 235 to co-operate with the administrator. If requested, the administrator must supply each person with instructions for the preparation of the statement and with the forms required for that purpose. The statement must be in the prescribed form and be verified by affidavit. The administrator may also require any person mentioned in s. 22 (see above) to submit an affidavit of concurrence stating either that he concurs in the statement, or that he is not in agreement with it, or that it is wrong or misleading, or that he does not have the necessary knowledge to enable him to concur. The verified copy of the statement together with the affidavits of concurrence must be filed in court by the
r. 2.13 administrator. If the administrator believes that disclosure of all or any part of the information in the statement would prejudice the conduct of the administration, he may apply to the court for an order that all or part of the statement need not be filed in court, or that it be filed separately and not be open to inspection without the leave of the court. The court order may also relate to delivery of documents to the registrar of companies and to the disclosure of relevant information to other persons.

The statement of affairs must show particulars of the company's assets and liabilities, names and addresses of its creditors, the securities held by them and the date these securities were given. The reasonable expenses of preparing the statement will be paid by the administrator. If any person fails, without reasonable excuse, to comply with the obligation to submit a statement he will be liable to prosecution.

The administrator or, if he refuses, the court may at any time release a person from the obligation to make and submit a statement of affairs or may, either at the time of or after service of the notice of requirement, extend the period for preparation and submission of the statement. This power may be exercised at the administrator's own discretion or by the court on application. Even if the court believes there is insufficient cause shown, it may not dismiss such an application unless the applicant has had an opportunity to attend the court for an *ex parte* hearing of which he has been given at least seven days' notice. If the court decides to hear the application it must notify the applicant and he must give the administrator at least 14 days' notice of the hearing and of the grounds of his claim. The administrator may attend and give evidence at the hearing and/or file a written report on any matters he feels should be brought to the court's attention. A copy of the report must be sent to the applicant at least five days before the hearing. The applicant must pay his own costs and no allowance for them may be made out of the assets unless the court orders otherwise.

s. 22

r. 2.14

3.8.2 The administrator's statement of proposals

The administrator must prepare, within three months after the making of the administration order or such longer period as the court may allow, a statement of his proposals for achieving the purpose of the administration order and must annex to it the following:

s. 23

r. 2.16

(a) details relating to his appointment as administrator, the purposes for which an administration order was applied for and made, and any subsequent variation of those purposes;

(b) the names of the directors and secretary of the company;

(c) an account of the circumstances giving rise to the application for an administration order;

(d) if a statement of affairs has been submitted, a copy or summary of it, with the administrator's comments, if any;

(e) if no statement of affairs has been submitted, details of the financial position of the company at the latest practicable date (which must, unless the court otherwise orders, be a date not earlier than that of the administration order);

(f) the manner in which the affairs of the company will be managed and its business financed, if the administrator's proposals are approved; and

(g) such other information (if any) as the administrator thinks necessary to enable creditors to decide whether or not to vote for the adoption of the proposals.

s. 23 Also within three months after the making of the administration order or such longer period as the court may allow, the administrator must deal with the statement of proposals in the following manner:

(a) send a copy to the registrar of companies;
(b) send a copy to all creditors;
(c) lay a copy before a meeting of the creditors (see 3.8.3 below); and
r. 2.17 (d) either send a copy to all members of the company or publish in the *Gazette*, and in the newspaper in which the administration order was advertised, a notice stating an address from which the members can obtain a free copy of the statement.

Failure to comply with the above renders the administrator liable to prosecution.

3.8.3 Creditors' and company meetings

s. 23 As stated in 3.8.2 above, the administrator must call a meeting of the creditors of the company within three months of the making of the administration order, or such longer period as the court may allow, in order to present his proposals for achieving the purpose or
r. 2.28 purposes of the administration order. Resolutions at a creditors' meeting are passed by a simple majority in value of those present and voting, in person or by proxy. The Act prescribes a minimum of 14
r. 2.19 days' notice for this meeting whilst the rules prescribe 21 days, an anomaly that will no doubt be corrected in due course.

Notice of the meeting must be sent to all creditors of the company of which the administrator is aware and who had claims against the company at the date of the administration order. The notice must specify the purpose of the meeting and include a statement dealing with entitlement to vote. Notice to attend must also be sent to any past or present directors of the company who, in the administrator's opinion, should be at the meeting.

The meeting must be held between 10 a.m. and 4 p.m. on a business
r. 2.20 day, unless the court directs otherwise, and will be chaired by the administrator or by his nominee, provided this nominee is a qualified insolvency practitioner or an employee of the administrator or his

firm and is experienced in insolvency matters. If, within 30 minutes of the time fixed for the meeting to start, there is no person present to act as chairman, the meeting will stand adjourned to the same time and place the following week or, if that is not a business day, to the next business day. The chairman may adjourn the meeting for up to 14 days from its original date and must do so if a resolution is passed to that effect if the majority for approval of the proposal is not achieved. r. 2.19(6) r. 2.19(7) r. 2.18(4)

To vote at a creditors' meeting a person must, by 12 noon on the preceding business day, have given the administrator written details of the debt he is claiming together with any further proof that the administrator may require. If he is unable to do this through no fault of his own the creditor may be allowed to vote at the chairman's discretion. The creditor's vote will be calculated on the balance of his liquidated and ascertained debt. If the debt is unliquidated or unascertained the chairman may estimate a minimum value for voting purposes and admit the claim accordingly. A secured creditor may vote on the unsecured amount (if any) of the debt and a person who has supplied the company with goods under a retention of title agreement may vote on the balance of the debt after the value of his retention rights, as estimated by him, has been deducted. Persons who have supplied goods to the company under hire-purchase, chattel leasing or conditional sale agreements may vote in respect of the amount of the debt due and payable at the date of the administration order with no account being taken of the value of any right under the agreement which has become exercisable solely by virtue of the administration proceedings. r. 2.22 r. 2.24 r. 2.26 r. 2.27

Subject to appeal to the court, the chairman may admit or reject a claim of entitlement to vote. If the appeal is successful the court may order that another meeting be summoned or make any other order as it thinks just. If the claim against the chairman's decision relates to a meeting called to consider the administrator's proposals, the appeal must be lodged within 28 days of delivery of the administrator's report. r. 2.23

The administrator must summon meetings of the creditors if requested to do so by one-tenth in value of the company's creditors or if he is directed to do so by the court. If the creditors' request is valid the administrator must call a meeting within 35 days, giving 21 days' notice. Unless it is resolved otherwise, the cost of these meetings will be borne by the requisitioning creditors and, as a further deterrent to unreasonable requests, the administrator has the power to require the requisitioning creditors to pay a deposit before he calls the meeting. s. 17(3) r. 2.21

If the administrator summons a meeting of the company's r. 2.31

members it will be called and conducted as if it were a general meeting of the company but the administrator or a qualified person nominated by him will be chairman.

3.8.4 Consideration of administrator's proposals

s. 24 The creditors may approve the proposals either in their entirety or with such modifications as are consented to by the administrator. At the conclusion of the meeting the administrator must report its result
r. 2.30(1) to the court and give notice of it to every creditor who received notice
r. 2.30(2) of the meeting and to any other creditor of whom he has since become aware. Should the meeting refuse to approve the proposals, the court may discharge the administration order and make such consequential provision as it thinks fit, or adjourn the hearing conditionally or unconditionally, or make an interim order or any other order that it thinks fit. Should the administration order be discharged, the administrator must, within 14 days after the order effecting the discharge, send an office copy of that order to the registrar of companies. Failure to do so without reasonable excuse will result in criminal liability being imposed on the administrator.

s. 25 During the course of the administration the administrator may propose to make substantial revisions to the approved proposals, in which case he must prepare a statement of his proposed revisions and deal with it in the same manner as the statement in 3.8.2 above except that no copy need be sent to the registrar of companies. Unless the creditors' meeting held to consider the revised proposals approves the administrator's proposed revisions, these revisions must not be implemented. Although the meeting has the power to approve subject to modifications, each modification must be consented to by the administrator. Subject to the above variations, the creditors' meeting must be conducted according to the rules laid down for creditors' meetings generally (see 3.8.3 above) and, within 14 days of its conclusion, notice of the result of the meeting must be given by the administrator to the registrar of companies, to every creditor who received notice and to any other creditor of whom the administrator has since become aware.

3.8.5 Creditors' committee

s. 26 If the creditors' meeting approves the proposals with or without modification it may, if it wishes, establish a creditors' committee
r. 2.32 comprising three to five elected creditors whose claims had been
r. 2.37 accepted. This may include a body corporate, which must act through a duly appointed representative to whom it must give a letter of authority that the chairman of the committee may inspect. Any creditor who complies with these requirements may be represented

by another unless that other is a body corporate, or an undischarged bankrupt or is subject to a composition or arrangement with his own creditors. r. 2.37(4)

When at least three of the proposed members of the committee have agreed to act, the administrator will issue a certificate of its due constitution, which he must file in the court. When this has been done the committee will come into existence and will be able to act. The first meeting must be called by the administrator no later than three months after it has been established and subsequent meetings must be called within 21 days of a request by a member or his representative or at such time as the committee itself resolves. The administrator must give seven days' written notice of the venue of the meeting to every committee member or his representative and the meeting will be valid if all members have received this notice and at least two are present or represented. The administrator or his nominee acts as chairman and resolutions are passed by a simple majority of those present and voting, each member having one vote. The administrator has the power to instigate a postal vote and, unless within seven days a member requires the summoning of a meeting to consider the proposed resolution, it will be passed if a majority of the committee write to the administrator expressing their approval. r. 2.33 r. 2.34(3) r. 2.36 r. 2.35 r. 2.42 r. 2.43

The committee's function is to assist the administrator. It has the power to require the administrator to attend before it at any reasonable time and to furnish it with such information in relation to the carrying out of his functions as it may reasonably require. The administrator must be given seven days' notice in writing signed by a majority of the committee. r. 2.34 s. 26(2) r. 2.44(1)

The fact that a creditor is a member of the committee does not stop him from dealing with the company during the administration provided he acts in good faith and that any transactions are for value. Transactions in bad faith or not for value may be set aside by the court on the application of any interested person. r. 2.46

A committee member may be removed by resolution at a creditors' meeting called on 14 days' notice and will automatically be removed if he becomes bankrupt; or compounds or arranges with his creditors; or if he stops being, or is found never to have been, a creditor; or if he misses three consecutive committee meetings (unless the third of these meetings resolves otherwise). If a member is removed because of bankruptcy, his trustee in bankruptcy will replace him as a member. A member may resign by giving notice in writing to the administrator. The vacancy on the committee may be filled by the administrator appointing another creditor with the consent of the majority of the other members. Provided the numbers do not fall below three, however, the vacancy need not be filled r. 2.40 r. 2.38 r. 2.41

provided the administrator and a majority of remaining committee members so agree.

3.8.6 General duties

r. 2.52 The administrator must prepare an abstract of receipts and payments for each six-month period that he acts and for the final period up to ceasing to act. These accounts must be sent to the court, the registrar of companies and to each member of the creditors' committee within two months after the end of each period. The two-month period may be extended by the court on the administrator's application. Failure to comply with these requirements will render the administrator liable to a fine.

r. 2.56 He must issue a certificate in the terms of the Value Added Tax Act 1983, s. 22(3)(b) (as amended by the Finance Act 1985, s. 32) if he concludes that the company is insolvent for the purposes of the 1983 Act. Within three months of his appointment or within two months of issuing the certificate (whichever is the later) the administrator must give notice of the issue of the certificate to all unsecured creditors of whom he is aware and who he knows have supplied the company, with a charge to VAT, at any time before his appointment. Thereafter, he must give notice to any such creditor of whom he becomes aware. The administrator has a duty, on vacating office, to bring this rule to the attention of the directors or, as the case may be, any successor of his as administrator.

During the currency of the administration the administrator must give all the company's creditors a progress report within 14 days of the end of every six-month period beginning with the date of the approval of his proposals. He must also report when he vacates office unless the company thereupon goes into liquidation or unless he has been removed by the court or has ceased to be a qualified insolvency practitioner.

s. 233 Hitherto, certain monopoly suppliers of utility services have been able to insist on the payment of outstanding accounts due by the company before they would allow a supply to the office holder. This is now illegal under the Act but the supplier is entitled to require a personal guarantee from the administrator in respect of future supplies. The supplies are:

(a) a public supply of gas;
(b) a supply of electricity by an electricity board;
(c) a supply of water by statutory water undertakers,
(d) a supply of telecommunication services by a public telecommunications operator.

A number of matters relating to events and malpractices before the commencement of the administration are common to both administrators and liquidators. These matters are set out in chapter 7.6 under the following headings:

(a) transactions at an undervalue and preferences (ss. 238 and 239);
(b) extortionate credit transactions (s. 244);
(c) avoidance of floating charges (s. 245);
(d) unenforceability of liens (s. 246).

The duty of an administrator to prepare a report for the Secretary of State on all directors of the company is dealt with in chapter 8.

3.9 Powers of an administrator

In general, an administrator has the power to do all things necessary for the management of the affairs, business and property of the company, but has specific powers under the Act to do the following: s. 14(1)

(a) Carry on the business of the company. sch. 1
(b) Take possession of the company's property. He is also empowered to effect and maintain insurances in respect of the business and property of the company, and to do anything necessary to realise the property.
(c) Raise or borrow money, and grant security over the company's property.
(d) Refer issues affecting the company to arbitration and make any arrangement or compromise on the company's behalf. He may also bring or defend any action or other legal proceedings in the name of and on behalf of the company.
(e) Appoint a solicitor, accountant or other professionally qualified person to assist him in the performance of his functions. He may also appoint an agent to do any business that he is unable to do himself or that can more conveniently be done by an agent.
(f) Present or defend a petition for the winding up of the company; call up any of the company's uncalled capital; change the situation of the company's registered office; use the company's seal and do all acts and execute in the name and on behalf of the company any deed, receipt or other document; draw, accept, make or endorse any bill of exchange or promissory note in the name and on behalf of the company.
(g) Rank and claim in bankruptcy, insolvency, sequestration or liquidation proceedings against a debtor of the company and receive

dividends and accede to trust deeds for the creditors of that debtor.

(h) Establish subsidiaries of the company and transfer to these or existing subsidiaries the whole or any part of the company's business.

(i) Grant or accept a surrender of a lease or tenancy of any of the company's property and take a lease or tenancy of any property required or convenient for the company's business.

(j) Employ and dismiss employees.

(k) Do all other things incidental to the exercise of all the above powers.

s. 14(2) In addition, the administrator has the authority to remove and appoint directors and to call any meeting of the members or creditors
s. 14(4) of the company and, unless the administrator gives consent either generally or in relation to particular cases, neither the company nor its officers can exercise any of their powers in such a way as to interfere with the administrator's functions. The administrator may also apply to the court for directions relating to any matter connected with the administration.

s. 14(5) In exercising his powers, the administrator is deemed to be acting as the company's agent and a person dealing with the administrator in good faith and for value does not have to inquire whether the administrator is acting within his powers.

3.9.1 Dealing with charged property

s. 15(1) The administrator also has power without requiring the court's consent to deal with certain charged property as if it were not
s. 15(3) charged. The securities that are affected by this power are those that, as created, were floating charges. When property is disposed of under this power, the proceeds of the disposal will become subject to a floating charge, which will have the same priority as that afforded to the original security.

s. 15(2) Disposal of any other charged property (not falling within the definition above), or any goods in the company's possession under a hire-purchase, conditional sale, chattel leasing or retention of title agreement, can be made only under an order of the court, unless the creditor involved agrees. Such an order may be made if, following an application by the administrator, the court is satisfied that the disposal, whether with or without other assets, would be likely to promote one or more of the purposes specified in the administration order. If the court is so satisfied, it may authorise the administrator
s. 15(7) to dispose of the property as if it were unencumbered. A copy of the order authorising the administrator to act in this way must be sent to the registrar of companies within 14 days of its being made. Failure
s. 15(8) to do so without reasonable excuse will render the administrator

liable to prosecution. The administrator must also give notice of the order to the holder of the security or owner of the goods. r. 2.51

The order authorising a disposal must require that the net proceeds of the disposal shall be applied towards the discharge of the sums secured by the security or payable under the hire purchase etc. agreement. If these proceeds are, in the court's opinion, less than would be realised on a sale in the open market by a willing vendor, the court will order that such sums as may be required to make good the deficiency shall also be applied in discharge of the security or in payment of the hire purchase etc. liability. The Act does not reveal where this money is to come from. If there are two or more securities involved, the money realised must be applied to the payment of those securities in the order of their priorities. s. 15(5) s. 15(6)

The power vested in the administrator to deal with charged property does not prejudice the protection afforded by s. 27 giving creditors the right to seek relief (see 3.10 below), nor secured creditors' rights under s. 11(3) (see 3.6 above).

3.10 Variation or discharge of an administration order

The administrator may, at any time, make an application to the court for the administration order to be either discharged or varied by the addition of another purpose. The application shall be made if it appears to the administrator that the purpose or each of the purposes specified in the order has been achieved or is incapable of achievement or if he has been instructed to make the application by a meeting of the company's creditors summoned for that purpose. On hearing the application, the court may discharge or vary the order and make such consequential provision as it thinks fit, adjourn the hearing conditionally or unconditionally, or make an interim order or any other order it sees fit. If the administration order is discharged or varied, the administrator must, within 14 days, send a copy of the order of discharge or variation to the registrar of companies. Failure to comply with this requirement without reasonable excuse will result in criminal sanctions being imposed on the administrator. s. 18

During the administration, a creditor or member of the company may petition the court if he considers that the company's affairs, business and property are being or have been managed by the administrator in a manner that is unfairly prejudicial to the interest of its creditors or members generally or of some part of its creditors or members (including at least himself). He may also petition if he considers that any actual or proposed act or omission of the administrator is or would be so prejudicial. Subject to certain restrictions, the court may make such order as it thinks fit for giving s. 27(1) s. 27(2) relief in respect of the matter complained of or adjourn the hearing conditionally or unconditionally, or make an interim order or any s. 27(4) other order that it thinks fit. Such an order may regulate the way the administrator manages the company in future, require the administrator to refrain from doing or continuing an act complained of or to do something he has omitted to do; require the summoning of a meeting of creditors or members to consider such matters as the court may direct; or discharge the administration order and make s. 27(6) such consequential provision as it thinks fit. An order discharging the administration order must be notified by the administrator to the registrar of companies within 14 days. Failure to do so will result in criminal liability.

s. 27(3) An order of the court shall not prejudice or prevent the implementation of any composition or scheme approved by the creditors' committee or any compromise or arrangement sanctioned under CA 1985, s. 425. Furthermore, where the application for the order is made more than 28 days after the approval of any proposals or revised proposals, the court order shall not prejudice or prevent their implementation.

3.11 Vacation of office by and release of an administrator

s. 19 An administrator may at any time be removed from office by order
r. 2.53(1) of the court and may give notice of his resignation to the court because of:

(a) ill health;
(b) his intention to cease practising as an insolvency practitioner;
(c) a conflict of interest or a change of personal circumstances precluding or making impracticable the further discharge by him of his duties.

r. 2.53(2) The administrator may resign on other grounds subject to the court giving consent.

r. 2.53(3) At least seven days' notice of his intention to resign must be given by the administrator to any continuing administrator or, in the absence of such a person, to the committee of creditors or, in the s. 19 absence of either, to the company and its creditors. The administrator must vacate his office if he ceases to be qualified to act as an insolvency practitioner in relation to the company or if the administration order is discharged. A person who has ceased to be the administrator of the company will have his release from the following times:

(a) if he has died, the release will date from the time at which notice of the death is given to the court. Such notice must be given by the administrator's personal representatives or, if he has a partner in a firm, by another partner who is qualified to act as an insolvency practitioner or is a member of any body recognised by the Secretary of State for the authorisation of insolvency practitioners, or by any person producing to the court the relevant death certificate or a copy of it; s. 20 r. 2.54

(b) in any other case, release will date from such time as the court may determine.

From the time of his release, a person will be discharged from liability for acts or omissions of his in relation to his conduct as administrator. However, if an administrator has misapplied or become accountable for any property of the company or has acted in breach of duty then the court may order the administrator to restore the property or contribute to the company's assets after he has been released. s. 20

Where at any time a person ceases to be the administrator of a company his remuneration and any expenses properly incurred by him shall be charged on and paid out of any property of the company that is in his custody or under his control at that time in priority to any security to which s. 15 then applies. Furthermore, any sums payable in respect of debts or liabilities incurred under contracts entered into or contracts of employment adopted while he or any predecessor was administrator shall be charged on and paid out of the property of the company in his custody or under his control at the time in priority to any charge for his remuneration and expenses. For these purposes, the administrator is not to be taken to have adopted a contract of employment by reason of anything done or omitted to be done within 14 days after his appointment. s. 19

Chapter 4

Administrative Receivers

4.1 Introduction

The Act introduced a new title for what had previously been referred to as a 'receiver and manager' and this person will now be called an
s. 29 'administrative receiver'. The Act defines an administrative receiver as being a receiver or manager of the whole, or substantially the whole, of a company's property appointed by or on behalf of the holders of any debentures of the company secured by a charge which, as created, was a floating charge, or by such a charge and one or more other securities.

The powers of a receiver have not hitherto been codified. The Act specifies the powers of an administrative receiver (similar to those of an administrator) and lays down detailed rules as to his appointment and vacation of office and the information that he must provide, and also gives limited powers to dispose of charged assets subject to approval by the court.

The essential element in the appointment of an administrative receiver is a floating charge and the administrative receiver's consequent ability to manage the company's business. If a receiver is appointed solely under a fixed charge he becomes receiver or manager of the property charged and has only the powers conferred by that charge or by the Law of Property Act 1925 which, in general terms, allow him only to deal with that property and any income arising therefrom. He has no power to deal with any property not comprised in the fixed charge and has no power to manage the company's business, and he is not required to be an insolvency practitioner. In view of the limited application of the Act to receivers or managers, and the need to refer to other legislation, this book does not deal further with this type of appointment.

The Act deals separately with receivership in England and Wales and receivership in Scotland. Although the procedures are not materially different, this book deals only with the procedures in England and Wales.

4.2 Appointment of an administrative receiver

The appointment of an administrative receiver must be accepted by him before the end of the business day following that on which the instrument of appointment is received by him or on his behalf. If accepted, the appointment is deemed to have been made at the time of receipt. The appointee, or someone acting on his behalf, must confirm the acceptance in writing to the appointer within seven days. The same rule applies in the case of the appointment of two or more persons as joint administrative receivers but their appointment will be effective only when each appointee, or someone acting on his behalf, has confirmed the acceptance in writing. If the appointment is discovered to be invalid the court may order the person by whom or on whose behalf the appointment was made to indemnify the appointee against any liability that arises because of the invalidity of the appointment. s. 33 r. 3.1(1) s. 34

4.2.1 Notification of appointment

Upon appointment, an administrative receiver must immediately send notice of his appointment to the company. The notice must state the registered name and number of the company; any other name under which the company has been registered or has traded in the preceding 12 months; details of the administrative receiver and the name of the appointer; brief details of the instrument under which the appointment was made; and a brief description of the assets of the company (if any) which remain outside the administrative receiver's control. Notice of the appointment must also be published in the *Gazette* and in such newspaper as the administrative receiver thinks most appropriate for ensuring that it comes to the notice of the company's creditors. s. 46 r. 3.2

Within 28 days of his appointment, unless the court otherwise directs, he must also send such a notice to all the creditors of the company in so far as he is aware of their addresses. However, an administrative receiver who is appointed to act with an existing administrative receiver, or in place of an administrative receiver who has ceased to act, must comply with the requirements as to notice only if the existing or previous administrative receiver has not already done so. If the company is in liquidation, the duty to give the required notices exists, notwithstanding that the administrative receiver and the liquidator are the same person, subject to the necessary modifications arising therefrom. Failure to comply with these requirements renders the administrative receiver liable to prosecution.

Every invoice, order for goods or business letter issued by or on behalf of the company or the administrative receiver or the s. 39

liquidator of the company, being a document on which the company's name appears, must contain a statement that an administrative receiver has been appointed. Failure to do this may make any officer, liquidator or administrative receiver liable to a fine.

It is the duty of the appointer to notify the appointment to the registrar of companies within seven days (CA 1985 s. 405).

4.2.2 Effect of appointment

Upon the appointment of an administrative receiver, the directors of the company lose their executive powers although they remain responsible for complying with their statutory duties in so far as they are able.

4.2.3 Application for administration

If an administrative receiver has been appointed, the court will not make an order for the appointment of an administrator unless the conditions in 3.4 (above) are satisfied. A copy of any petition for an
r. 2.6 administration order must be served on the administrative receiver and he has the right to appear at the hearing of the petition. If an
s. 11(1) administrator is appointed, the administrative receiver must vacate
s. 11(3) office, the effects of which are dealt with in 3.6 (above). When an administrator is in office it is not possible for an administrative receiver to be appointed.

4.3 Powers of an administrative receiver

s. 42 An administrative receiver will have the powers conferred on him by the debenture under which he was appointed. These powers are
sch. 1 deemed to include those specified in the Act (as applying both to an administrator and an administrative receiver) and enable him to do the following:

sch. 1 (a) Carry on the business of the company.

(b) Take possession of the company's property. He is also empowered to effect and maintain insurances in respect of the business and property of the company, and to do anything necessary to realise the property.

(c) Raise or borrow money, and grant security over the company's property.

(d) Refer issues affecting the company to arbitration and make any arrangement or compromise on the company's behalf. He may also bring or defend any action or other legal proceedings in the name of and on behalf of the company.

(e) Appoint a solicitor, accountant or other professionally qualified person to assist him in the performance of his functions. He may also appoint an agent to do any business that he is unable to do himself or that can more conveniently be done by an agent.

(f) Present or defend a petition for the winding up of the company; call up any of the company's uncalled capital; change the situation of the company's registered office; use the company's seal and do all acts and execute in the name and on behalf of the company any deed, receipt or other document; draw, accept, make or endorse any bill of exchange or promissory note in the name and on behalf of the company.

(g) Rank and claim in bankruptcy, insolvency, sequestration or liquidation proceedings against a debtor of the company and receive dividends and accede to trust deeds for the creditors of that debtor.

(h) Establish subsidiaries of the company and transfer to these or existing subsidiaries the whole or any part of the company's business.

(i) Grant or accept a surrender of a lease or tenancy of any of the company's property and take a lease or tenancy of any property required or convenient for the company's business.

(j) Employ and dismiss employees.

(k) Do all other things incidental to the exercise of all the above powers.

References in the above powers to 'property of the company' are to be construed as references to the property of which the administrative receiver is or, but for the appointment of some other person as the receiver of part of the company's property, would be the receiver or manager.

A person dealing with the administrative receiver of a company in good faith and for value shall not be concerned to inquire whether the administrative receiver is acting within his powers.

4.3.1 Dealing with charged property

The administrative receiver may apply to the court for an order s. 43
authorising him to dispose of any of the company's property that is subject to security as if it were uncharged. However, this power does not extend to any security held by the administrative receiver's appointer or to any security where that appointer has a prior charge. Also the power cannot extend to property that is, or would be, entirely outside the scope of the security under which the administrative receiver was appointed. Upon application by the administrative receiver, the court may authorise him to dispose of the assets if it is satisfied that the disposal would be likely to promote a more advantageous realisation of the company's assets than would otherwise be effected.

The order authorising the disposal must require that the net proceeds of such disposal be applied towards the discharge of the sums secured by the charge. If these proceeds are, in the court's opinion, less than would be realised on a sale in the open market by a willing vendor, the court will order that such sums as may be required to make good the deficiency shall also be applied in discharge of the security. If there are two or more charges involved, the money realised must be applied to the payment of these charges in the order of their priorities.

The administrative receiver has a duty to send a copy of the order authorising him to sell the secured property to the registrar of companies within 14 days of its being made. Failure to do so without reasonable excuse will render the administrative receiver liable to prosecution.

4.4 Duties of an administrative receiver

The duty of an administrative receiver is to manage the company's business and affairs and safeguard the assets under his control with a view to realising sufficient funds to discharge the company's indebtedness to his appointer. In the process he may be required to account to other secured creditors and he must deal with the preferential creditors of the company (see 4.4.5 below). When he has completed this task he will return the control of the company's business and assets to the company's directors, or to a liquidator if one has been appointed.

4.4.1 Statement of affairs

s. 47 On appointment, the administrative receiver must forthwith require the preparation and submission to him of a statement of affairs of the company by those persons he considers most qualified to make one.
r. 3.3 He must give each of these persons notice of his requirement and, if requested, give them instructions on the preparation of the statement and the forms required for that purpose. This statement must be verified by affidavit by the persons submitting it, and must show
s. 47(2) particulars of the company's assets and liabilities; names and addresses of its creditors; the securities held by them and the date these securities were given. It must be submitted within 21 days of the day after that on which the administrative receiver gives notice and must be made and submitted by the same persons as those listed in 3.8.1 (above).

The rules relating to affidavits of concurrence, release from duty to submit a statement and expenses of preparing the statement are the same as those that apply in an administration as set out in 3.8.1 (above).

A summary of the statement of affairs and the administrative receiver's comments on it (if any) must be included in the report to the company's creditors required in 4.4.2 (below) within three months of appointment. A copy of the statement of affairs and copies of any affidavits of concurrence must be sent to the registrar of companies at the same time as a copy of the report. If the statement of affairs is not then available a copy must be sent as soon as the administrative receiver obtains it. If the administrative receiver considers that disclosure of all or part of the statement of affairs would prejudice the receivership he may apply to the court for an order limiting disclosure. r. 3.8 r. 3.8(4)

An administrative receiver who is appointed to act with an existing administrative receiver or to replace a receiver who has ceased to act is obliged to obtain a statement of affairs unless this has already been done. If the company is in liquidation, the duty to require and submit a statement of affairs will still exist notwithstanding that the administrative receiver and the liquidator are the same person, subject to the necessary modifications arising therefrom. s. 46

4.4.2 Report to creditors

Within three months after his appointment, or such longer time as the court may allow, the administrative receiver must send a report to the registrar of companies, to any trustees for secured creditors of the company and, in so far as he is aware of their addresses, to all such creditors, containing information as to the following matters: s. 48

(a) the events leading up to his appointment so far as he is aware of them;

(b) the disposal or proposed disposal by him of any property of the company and the carrying on or proposed carrying on by him of any business of the company;

(c) the amounts of principal and interest payable to the debenture holder(s) by whom or on whose behalf he was appointed and the amounts payable to preferential creditors;

(d) the amount, if any, likely to be available for payment to other creditors;

(e) a summary of the statement of affairs made out and submitted to the administrative receiver and of his comments, if any, on it.

The report does not have to disclose any information that would seriously prejudice the receivership.

Again within three months of his appointment or such longer time as the court may allow, the administrative receiver must send a copy s. 48

of the report to the company's unsecured creditors in so far as he is
r. 3.8 aware of their addresses. Alternatively, he must publish a notice in the newspaper in which his appointment was advertised giving an address to which the unsecured creditors may write for copies of the report to be sent to them free of charge. In either case, unless the court otherwise directs, the administrative receiver must lay a copy of the report before a meeting of the unsecured creditors summoned for the purpose. The court will give a direction releasing the administrative receiver from this duty only if his report states that he intends to apply for the direction and if a copy of the report is sent to the unsecured creditors of the company or a notice is published in the newspaper in which the original appointment of the administrative receiver was advertised, not less that 14 days before the hearing of the application.

s. 48 If the company has gone or goes into liquidation, the administrative receiver must, within seven days of the submission of his report to the registrar of companies or, if later, the nomination or appointment of the liquidator, send a copy of the report to the liquidator. If the report is sent to the liquidator within three months of the administrative receiver's appointment, the administrative receiver is released from the obligations to the unsecured creditors regarding the report and calling a meeting. If the report has already been made by another administrative receiver before the present one is appointed a further report does not have to be submitted. If, however, an administrative receiver does have to submit a report and fails to do so without reasonable excuse he will be liable to prosecution.

4.4.3 Creditors' meeting

r. 3.9 If summoning the creditors' meeting referred to above, the administrative receiver must do so on at least 14 days' notice to all those creditors identified in the statement of affairs or of whom the administrative receiver is aware and who have claims against the company at the date of his appointment. The notice must state that those creditors whose claims are wholly secured are not entitled to attend or be represented at the meeting. Notice of the venue of the meeting must be published in the newspaper in which the administrative receiver's appointment was advertised and all notices must contain a statement dealing with creditors' voting rights. The meeting must be held between 10.00 a.m. and 4.00 p.m. at a place that takes into account the convenience of the creditors, and a proxy form must be sent out with the notice.

r. 3.10 The meeting must be chaired by the administrative receiver or his nominee, provided this nominee is a qualified insolvency practitioner or is an employee of the administrative receiver or his firm and is experienced in insolvency matters. To vote at a creditors' meeting a person must, by 12 noon on the preceding business day, have given the administrative receiver written details of the debt he is claiming, together with any further proof that the administrative receiver may require. If he is unable to do this through no fault of his own the creditor may, at the chairman's discretion, be allowed to vote. A creditor's vote will be calculated on the balance of his liquidated and ascertained debt. If the debt is unliquidated or unascertained the chairman may estimate a minimum value for voting purposes and admit the claim accordingly. A secured creditor may vote on the unsecured amount (if any) of the debt based on his own estimated valuation of the security. r. 3.11

Subject to appeal to the court, the chairman may admit or reject a claim of entitlement to vote. If the appeal is successful, the court may order that another meeting be summoned or make any other order as it thinks just. If the chairman is unsure whether or not a claim should be admitted he must mark it as objected to and allow the creditor to vote subject to his vote subsequently being declared invalid if the objection to the claim is sustained. r. 3.12

The quorum at a creditors' meeting is at least three creditors who are entitled to vote and, if the number of creditors does not exceed three, all must be present for the meeting to be valid. A single person will constitute a quorum provided either that he is a creditor or a representative under CA 1985, s. 375, he is entitled to vote and holds sufficient proxies to ensure that, with his own vote, at least three creditors are represented or that he is the chairman, or any other person, and holds that number of proxies. Even if there is not a quorum the meeting may not be adjourned unless the chairman decides that an adjournment is desirable. If he does so decide, he may adjourn to a date, time and place as he thinks fit. If there is not a quorum and a meeting is not adjourned it is deemed to have been duly summoned and held. Resolutions at a creditors' meeting are passed by a simple majority of those present and voting in person or by proxy. r. 3.13 r. 3.14 r. 3.15

4.4.4 Creditors' committee

The meeting may resolve to establish a creditors' committee of three to five elected creditors whose claims have been accepted. The function of the committee is to assist the administrative receiver in carrying out his functions and to act in such manner as may be agreed from time to time. It has no power to supervise or direct the administrative receiver but a majority of the members may give him seven days' written notice to appear before it and to give it such r. 3.16 r. 3.18 s. 49 r. 3.28

information as it may reasonably require.

This committee may include a body corporate, which must act through a duly appointed representative to whom it must give a letter of authority that the chairman may inspect. Any creditor who complies with these requirements may be represented by another person unless that person is a body corporate, or an undischarged bankrupt, or is subject to a composition or arrangement with his own creditors. A person may not act as the representative of more than one committee member on the same committee nor may a person act as both a committee member and a representative of another member.

When three of the proposed members of a committee have agreed
r. 3.17 to act, the administrative receiver will issue and send to the registrar of companies a certificate of its due constitution. The committee will
r. 3.18 not be able to act until this certificate is issued. The first meeting must be called by the administrative receiver no later than three months after it has been established. Subsequent meetings must be called within 21 days of a request by a committee member or his representative or at such time as the committee itself resolves. The administrative receiver must give seven days' written notice of the venue of the meeting to every committee member or his
r. 3.19 representative. The chair will be taken by the administrative receiver or his qualified nominee and the meeting will be valid if due notice
r. 3.20 has been given to all members and at least two are present or
r. 3.26 represented. Each member of the committee has one vote and resolutions are passed by a simple majority of members present or
r. 3.27 represented. The receiver has the power to instigate a postal vote, and, unless within seven days a member requires the summoning of a meeting to consider the proposed resolution, it will be passed if a majority of the committee writes to the administrative receiver expressing approval.

r. 3.30 The fact that a creditor is a member of the committee does not stop his dealing with the company during the receivership provided he acts in good faith and any transactions are for value. Transactions in bad faith or not for value may be set aside by the court on the application of any interested person.

r. 3.24 A committee member may be removed by a creditors' meeting provided at least 14 days' notice has been given of the intention to
r. 3.23 move the resolution. A member will be removed automatically if he becomes bankrupt or compounds or arranges with his creditors; or if he stops being or is found never to have been a creditor; or if he misses three consecutive meetings (unless the third of these meetings resolves otherwise). If a member is removed because of his bankruptcy, his trustee in bankruptcy will replace him as member. A member may resign by giving notice in writing to the administrative

receiver. Any vacancy on the committee may be filled by the administrative receiver appointing another qualified creditor with the consent of the majority of the other members. Provided the members do not fall below three, however, a vacancy need not be filled provided the administrative receiver and a majority of the remaining members so agree. r. 3.22

4.4.5 Preferential creditors

An administrative receiver, by virtue of his appointment under a floating charge, has a duty to pay a company's preferential creditors out of the assets which are subject to that floating charge in priority to any claims for principal or interest due to the holder of that charge. s. 40

The categories of preferential creditors (money owed to the Inland Revenue for income tax deducted at source; VAT, car tax, betting and gaming duties; social security and pension scheme contributions; remuneration of employees) are the same in administrative receivership as they are in liquidations and are listed more fully in 7.8.3. s. 386

4.4.6 General duties

The administrative receiver must prepare an abstract of receipts and payments for each 12-month period that he acts and for the final period up to ceasing to act. These accounts must be sent to the registrar of companies, the company, each member of the creditors' committee, and to the person who appointed him. Failure to comply with these requirements renders the administrative receiver liable to a fine. r. 3.32

As with the administrator, the administrative receiver also has a duty to issue a certificate in the terms of the Value Added Tax Act 1983, s. 22(3)(b) (see 3.8.6 above). r. 3.36

The duty of an administrative receiver to prepare a report for the Secretary of State on all directors of the company is dealt with in chapter 8.

4.5 Rights and liabilities of an administrative receiver

Unless and until the company to which he is appointed goes into liquidation, the administrative receiver is deemed to be the company's agent. He is personally liable on any contract entered into by him in the carrying out of his functions, unless the contract provides otherwise. He is also personally liable on any contract of employment that he adopts in his capacity as administrative receiver, although he will not be taken to have adopted such a contract by s. 44

reason of anything done or omitted to be done within 14 days after his appointment. In respect of liabilities properly incurred by him, the administrative receiver is entitled to an indemnity out of the company's assets. This right is in addition to the administrative
s. 44(3) receiver's other rights to be indemnified. The Act, however, does not limit his liability on contracts entered into or adopted without authority nor does it confer any rights to indemnity in respect of that liability.

Hitherto, certain monopoly suppliers of utility services have been able to insist on the payment of outstanding accounts due by the company before they would allow a supply to the office holder. This is now illegal under the Act but the supplier is entitled to require a personal guarantee from the administrative receiver in respect of future supplies. The supplies are:

(a) a public supply of gas;
(b) a supply of electricity by an electricity board;
(c) a supply of water by statutory water undertakers;
(d) a supply of telecommunication services by a public telecommunications operator.

4.6 Vacation of office by an administrative receiver

s. 45 An administrative receiver may at any time be removed from office by, and only by, order of the court. He may resign his office by giving
r. 3.33 seven days' notice to the person by whom he was appointed and to the company or, if it is in liquidation, to the liquidator. No notice need be given if the administrative receiver resigns following the making of an administration order. If an administrative receiver ceases to be qualified to act as an insolvency practitioner he must
r. 3.34 vacate office and, if he dies, the person by whom he was appointed must, as soon as he becomes aware of the death, give notice of it to the registrar of companies and to the company (or its liquidator if relevant).

Where the administrative receiver vacates office (other than by death) he must notify the following:

(a) The registrar of companies (within 14 days). Notification is required both by s. 45(4) of the Act and by CA 1985, s. 405. The same
r. 3.35 form (405(2)) may be used to cover both requirements. Failure to notify the registrar of companies without reasonable excuse will render the administrative receiver liable to prosecution.
(b) The liquidator (if any).
(c) The creditors' committee (if any).

Following his vacation of office, an administrative receiver's claims to remuneration and any properly incurred expenses, and any indemnity to which he is entitled out of the assets of the company, shall be charged on and paid out of any property of the company which is in his custody or under his control at that time, in priority to any security held by the person by or on whose behalf he was appointed.

Chapter 5

Voluntary Liquidation

5.1 Introduction

There are two kinds of voluntary liquidation:

(a) a members' voluntary liquidation—which operates where the company is solvent and which is controlled largely by the company's members; and

(b) a creditors' voluntary liquidation—which operates in circumstances where the company is insolvent and in relation to which, in broad terms, the wishes and interests of the creditors are generally paramount.

This chapter is set out under the following headings:

5.2 Members' voluntary liquidation
5.3 Creditors' voluntary liquidation
5.4 Matters applicable to both types of voluntary liquidation

5.2 Members' voluntary liquidation

s. 84 A company may be put into liquidation at any time if the members pass a special resolution to that effect. If the term of the company's life under its articles expires or if an event occurs as a result of which the articles require the company to be wound up, the liquidation may commence on the passing of an ordinary resolution.

5.2.1 Declaration of solvency

It is essential in a members' voluntary liquidation that a declaration of solvency is made. If no such declaration is or can be made the liquidation will be a creditors' voluntary liquidation.

s. 89 The directors (or a majority if more than two) must make a statutory declaration of solvency during the five weeks *before* the date of the resolution to wind up or, if *on* the date of resolution, immediately before the resolution. The declaration must include a statement of assets and liabilities as at the latest practicable date and state that within 12 months of the commencement of the liquidation (i.e., the resolution date) the company will be able to pay all its creditors in full (including interest defined in s. 189(4)). It is an offence for directors to make the declaration without reasonable grounds and if the debts are not paid in accordance with the declaration there is a presumption that there were no reasonable grounds. s. 89(4) and (5)

5.2.2 Appointment of liquidator

The ordinary rules of company law and the regulations of the company's articles govern the convening and holding of the members' meeting (contents of the notice, period of notice, unanimously signed resolutions and filing). If the resolution to wind up is not passed within five weeks after the date of the declaration of solvency it is of no effect.

The liquidator is appointed by an ordinary resolution (there may, as in all liquidations, be joint and several liquidators). The chairman of the meeting must certify the appointment, after the nominee has stated his qualification and consent to act, and send the certificate to the liquidator who keeps it as part of his records. The following filing and notification requirements apply following the passing of the resolution to wind up: r. 4.139

(a) a special resolution must be filed with the registrar of companies within 15 days (CA 1985, s. 380);

(b) the declaration of solvency must be filed with the registrar of companies within 15 days; s. 89(3)

(c) notice of the resolution must be advertised in the *Gazette* within 14 days; s. 85(1)

(d) notice of the liquidator's appointment must be published in the *Gazette* and delivered to the registrar of companies within 14 days; s. 109

(e) all creditors must be notified of the liquidator's appointment within 28 days. r. 4.139(4)

5.2.3 Administration of the liquidation

The liquidator's function is to wind up the affairs of the company and distribute its assets. As the company is solvent all the creditors will be paid in full and there will be a surplus for distribution amongst the members. This surplus is distributed according to the rights and interests of the members in accordance with the company's articles and may be distributed in cash or in specie. s. 107

s. 91(2) The directors' powers cease on the appointment of the liquidator unless the members or the liquidator decide otherwise.

s. 93 If the liquidation continues for more than one year the liquidator
must summon a meeting of the members within three months of the
s. 192 end of that year and every succeeding year and present an account of
r. 223 his conduct of the liquidation. He must also, within 30 days after the
end of the first year and thereafter at six-monthly intervals send a statement, in duplicate, to the registrar of companies, of his receipts and payments. The penalty for non-compliance is a fine.

The powers and duties of a liquidator in a members' voluntary liquidation are referred to in 5.4 (below) and in chapter 7 (Rules common to all liquidations).

5.2.4 Conversion to creditors' voluntary liquidation

ss. 95 If the liquidator forms the opinion that the company will be unable
and 96 to pay its debts and the statutory interest in full within the period stated by the directors in the declaration of solvency he must seek to have the voluntary liquidation converted into a creditors' voluntary liquidation and must do the following:

s. 95(2)(a) (a) Summon a creditors' meeting within 28 days of forming his opinion.

s. 95(2)(b) (b) Give creditors seven days' notice by post of the meeting, enclosing proxy forms.

s. 95(2)(c) (c) Gazette that notice and advertise it in two newspapers
s. 95(5) circulating in every locality in which the company had its principal
place of business during the six months before resolving upon the
s. 95(6) members' voluntary liquidation (or registered office if there was no
such principal place of business).

s. 95(2)(d) (d) Furnish creditors (free of charge) with information reasonably required, notifying them of this right in the notice of the meeting.

s. 95(3) (e) Prepare a statement of affairs and lay it before the creditors'
meeting. The statement which will include particulars of assets, debts
s. 95(4) and liabilities, names and address of the creditors and dates and
r. 4.34(1) details of any securities held by creditors must be delivered to the
r. 4.34(2) registrar of companies within seven days after the creditors' meeting.

s. 95(3)(c) (f) Preside at the creditors' meeting.

Once the above meeting is held the effect is as if the declaration of solvency had not been made.

5.2.5 Finalisation of the liquidation

s. 94 When he has fully wound up the affairs of the company the liquidator must call a general meeting of the company laying before it an account of the conduct of the liquidation and how the company's property has been disposed of. The meeting must be called by advertisement in the *Gazette* at least one month before the meeting. Within one week after the meeting the liquidator must file a copy of the account with the registrar of companies together with a return of the holding of, or (if appropriate) the lack of a quorum at, the meeting. Breach of this duty renders the liquidator liable to a fine.

Release of the liquidator takes effect as follows: s. 171

(a) resignation—when notice is given to registrar of companies; r. 4.144

(b) removal by company meeting—when notice is given to registrar of companies; s. 173(2)

(c) removal by court or as a result of ceasing to be an insolvency practitioner—when Secretary of State determines; s. 173(2)

(d) on completion—when returns of the final meeting are filed with the registrar of companies.

5.3 Creditors' voluntary liquidation

If there is a resolution to wind up the company and no declaration of solvency has been or can be made, the winding up is a creditors' voluntary winding up. The date of the resolution is the commencement of liquidation. The resolution will be an extraordinary one to the effect that the company cannot by reason of its liabilities continue in business and that it is advisable to wind up. s. 86 s. 84(1)(c)

5.3.1 Commencement of liquidation

The procedure is as follows:

(a) The company must give at least seven days' notice to the creditors of a meeting, which must be held within 14 days of the date of the resolution to wind up. Proxy forms must be sent with the notice and creditors wishing to be entitled to vote must submit such proof of debt as is specified in the notices. The meeting must commence between 10.00 a.m. and 4.00 p.m. and be held at a place that has regard to the convenience of the people entitled to attend. s. 98(1)(a) and (b) r. 4.60

(b) The notice must be published in the *Gazette* and advertised in two local newspapers appropriate to every locality of the company's principal place of business during the six months prior to the resolution to wind up the company (failing a principal place of business the locality of the registered office suffices). s. 98(1)(c) and s. 98(3), (4) and (5)

(c) The notice must state either: s. 98(2)

(i) the name and address of a qualified insolvency practitioner who can, free of charge, supply such information about the company's affairs as the creditors may reasonably require; or

(ii) a place in the locality where during the two business days before the creditors' meeting a list of creditors' names and addresses may be inspected free of charge.

s. 99 (d) The directors must make out a statement of affairs in the
r. 4.34 prescribed form which must be verified by affidavit. It must be laid before the creditors' meeting and then delivered to the appointed liquidator who, within seven days of his appointment, must deliver it to the registrar of companies. These duties are an expense of the
r. 4.38 liquidation.

(e) The directors must choose one of their number to preside at
r. 4.53 the creditors' meeting. Business at the meeting is restricted to the appointment of a liquidator and a liquidation committee unless the chairman otherwise decides.

s. 166 (f) If the members have nominated a liquidator he must attend the meeting of creditors. He must report to the meeting any exercise of his powers.

(g) The conduct of the creditors' meeting is with minor exceptions similar to that in compulsory liquidation as set out in chapter 6. Resolutions are passed by a majority in value.

s. 100 (h) Appointment of liquidator—the contributories and creditors may both nominate a liquidator but, if different liquidators are nominated, the creditors' nomination prevails unless the court otherwise orders on application within seven days by any director, creditor or contributory. The chairman of the meeting, on receipt of
r. 4.101 the appointee's written statement of qualification and consent to act, certifies the appointment and gives the certificate to the appointee.

(i) The winding-up resolution must be filed with the registrar of companies within 15 days, and notice of the resolution must be gazetted within 14 days. The liquidator must deliver a notice of his
s. 109 appointment to the registrar of companies within 14 days and advertise the appointment in the *Gazette* also within 14 days, as well
r. 4.49 as in a newspaper appropriate to the creditors. The liquidator must also, within 28 days of the creditors' meeting send a summary of the statement of affairs and a report of the meeting to the company's creditors.

s. 103 (j) The powers of the directors cease on the appointment of a liquidator unless the liquidation committee otherwise decides.

The reasonable and necessary expenses incurred in summoning, advertising and holding a creditors' meeting under s. 98 are an expense of the liquidation.

5.3.2 Liquidator's powers and duties

The liquidator has the following powers and duties:

(a) Where a liquidator is appointed by the company before the s. 166
creditors have met and nominated a liquidator, the company's nominee must not, without court sanction, dispose of assets other than perishables or things likely to diminish in value if not disposed s. 166(3)
of immediately. He can, however, act to take assets into his custody or control or to protect them. These rules are intended to put an end to the previous practice of 'Centrebinding'.

(b) He must notify the liquidation committee of any disposals of s. 165(6),
assets to company associates. s. 249 and

(c) He can disclaim onerous property. s. 435

(d) He can apply to the court for directions.

(e) He can call annual meetings of creditors and contributories and make annual returns.

(f) See also rules applicable in both kinds of voluntary winding up, and chapter 7 (Rules common to all liquidations).

5.3.3 The liquidation committee

The creditors may appoint a liquidation committee consisting of up s. 101
to five creditors, and may allow the contributories also to appoint up to five members. The creditors may, however, subject to any s. 101(3)
contrary court order, disqualify any of the contributories' appointees. The rules governing the membership and conduct of the liquidation committee are broadly similar to those applicable in a compulsory liquidation (see 6.8).

5.3.4 Finalisation of the liquidation

When the company's affairs are fully wound up, the liquidator must s. 106
call creditors' and contributories' meetings to lay before them an account of the conduct of, and disposal of assets in, the liquidation and an explanation of it (the creditors may question him on any r. 4.126(2)
matter in the account). The meetings are called by advertisement in the *Gazette* at least one month before the meeting; and 28 days' s. 106(2)
notice must be given to all creditors who have proved their debts. Within one week after the completion of both meetings the account s. 106(3)
must be filed with the registrar of companies (accompanied by a return of the holding of the meetings).

Release of the liquidator takes effect as follows: s. 171

(a) resignation—when notice is given to registrar of companies;

(b) removal by creditors' meeting—when notice is given to s. 173(2)
registrar of companies;

s. 173(2) (c) removal by court or as a result of ceasing to be an insolvency practitioner—when Secretary of State determines;

s. 173(2) (d) on completion—when returns of the final meeting are filed with the registrar of companies.

r. 4.126 A creditors' meeting may resolve against the release of the liquidator in which case he must obtain his release from the Secretary of State.

5.4 Matters applicable to both types of voluntary liquidation

The following matters are applicable in both a members' and a creditors' voluntary liquidation:

s. 108 (a) The court may appoint a liquidator if there is no liquidator acting.

(b) Debts must be paid *pari passu* except where the Act makes debts preferential and any surplus shall be distributed according to the contributories' rights and interests in the company (unless the articles deal differently with such surplus). Expenses rank before debts (s. 115).

s. 110 (c) To facilitate takeovers and mergers, the whole or part of the company's business or property can be transferred by the liquidator in consideration of shares, policies or like interests in, or profits of or benefits in the transferee company. In a members' voluntary liquidation the liquidator needs a general or specific sanction of a special resolution of the company; in a creditors' voluntary winding up sanction is provided by the liquidation committee or the court. Members who did not vote for the special resolution may within seven days of the resolution leave written notice of dissent at the registered office requiring the liquidator to abandon the proposal or
s. 111 to buy out the dissenter. If he proceeds with the transaction the liquidator must raise the money to buy out dissenters before dissolving the company (in such manner as the general meeting by special resolution decides).

Creditors may interfere if the scheme appears to compel them to look for payment of their debts otherwise than from the assets in the liquidation.

s. 112 (d) The liquidator or any creditor or contributory may ask the court to exercise any powers which are exercisable in a compulsory liquidation. Copies of the court's order must be sent to the liquidator and the registrar of companies.

(e) Where no liquidator has been nominated or appointed by the company, the directors may not act without the sanction of the court except to protect the assets or dispose of perishables or goods likely to diminish in value if not disposed of, or to see that meetings and a statement of affairs in relation to a creditors' voluntary liquidation are duly dealt with. s. 114

(f) A voluntary liquidation may be converted into a compulsory liquidation. If a contributory applies, the court must be satisfied that contributories' rights will be prejudiced by a voluntary liquidation. s. 116

(g) After commencement of the liquidation no alteration can be made to the status of the company's members and any transfer of shares requires the sanction of the liquidator. s. 88

The creditors may appear on a winding-up petition and the court will take into account their views. The onus of showing that the voluntary liquidation ought not to continue lies on the petitioning creditor (per Diplock LJ in *Swain J.D. Ltd* [1965] 1 WLR 909). The creditors' wishes will be considered according to their 'number, value and quality' (*Re Lowestoft Traffic Services Co. Ltd* (1985) 2 BCC 98,945). If the voluntary liquidator is biased and a case for investigation arises (*Re Palmer Marine Surveys Ltd* [1986] 1 WLR 573) or even if, without criticism of the voluntary liquidator, there may be understandable disquiet among the creditors (*Re Lowestoft Traffic Services Co. Ltd*) the court will grant the order. If clear benefits will flow from continuing the voluntary liquidation (e.g., savings of costs and time) and the petitioner adduces no evidence of possible harm the court will refuse the petition.

If a winding-up order is made against the company the liquidator appointed by the court will take custody of all the company's property. The winding-up order would probably direct that the voluntary liquidator be released.

(h) The liquidator may resign on account of ill health, cessation of practice, conflict of interest, or personal circumstances on the grounds that continuation is impossible or impracticable. s. 171(5) r. 4.142 r. 4.108

In order to resign, a liquidator must call a meeting of members, in a members' voluntary liquidation, or creditors, in a creditors' voluntary liquidation (although the creditors may refuse to accept the resignation, in which case the liquidator may apply to the court). r. 4.111 At either meeting the liquidator must present a summary of his receipts and payments. Resignation becomes effective once the liquidator has notified the registrar of companies.

Application may be made to the court for the removal of the liquidator. If the application is successful the court gives the s. 171(2) r. 4.143

liquidator two copies of the removal order, one of which is for transmission to the registrar of companies (accompanied by a notice of ceasing to act).

Chapter 6

Compulsory Liquidation

6.1 Introduction

Compulsory liquidation arises where the court orders that a company be wound up following the presentation of a petition for such an order. Whilst voluntary liquidation may be quicker and less expensive than the compulsory process, the latter is very necessary where, for example, the company may refuse to admit its insolvency and persists in trading, to the obvious detriment of its creditors or where an administrative receiver is unable to make recoveries in respect of voidable preferences or transactions at an undervalue and the creditors wish to pursue such a course. No less important, in the case of small private companies, minority shareholders who petition for relief under CA 1985, ss. 459 to 461, from unfairly prejudicial behaviour in the conduct of their company's affairs may wish to petition in the alternative for a winding-up order. The new flexibility available to the official receiver to decide not to hold creditors' and contributories' meetings and to ask for early dissolution where the assets are insignificant and no further investigation is warranted may help to produce a more efficient compulsory liquidation service.

The law applicable to compulsory liquidation will be considered under the following headings:

6.2 Grounds upon which a petition may be based
6.3 Persons who may petition
6.4 Procedure for presenting a petition
6.5 Consequences of presenting a petition
6.6 The winding-up order and its consequences
6.7 Liquidators
6.8 Liquidation committee
6.9 Control of the liquidation by the court
6.10 Winding-up unregistered companies
6.11 Vacation of office of liquidator

6.2 Grounds upon which a petition may be based

s. 122 The grounds upon which a winding-up petition may be based are:

(a) a special resolution to wind up compulsorily has been carried by the company;

(b) a company registered as public on incorporation has not been issued with a certificate under CA 1985, s. 117 (public company share capital requirements), and more than a year has expired since it was so registered;

(c) the company is an old public company within the meaning of the Companies Consolidation (Consequential Provisions) Act 1985, s. 1;

(d) the company does not commence its business within a year from its incorporation or suspends its business for a whole year;

(e) the number of members is less than two;

(f) the company is unable to pay its debts;

(g) the court is of the opinion that it is just and equitable that the company should be wound up;

s. 124(4) and CA 1985, s. 440 (h) from a report of inspectors under CA 1985, s. 437, or from information or documents obtained under CA 1985, ss. 447 or 448, it appears to the Secretary of State that it is expedient in the public interest that the company be wound up provided that the court thinks it just and equitable to do so (see 6.3.5).

These grounds are considered in more detail below.

6.2.1 Special resolution by the company

This is most uncommon in practice since a company can always be put into voluntary liquidation by a similar resolution. The court would, perhaps, need to be satisfied that some advantage would accrue to the company or its creditors from going through the compulsory process.

6.2.2 Failure within a year of incorporation to obtain a certificate under CA 1985, s. 117

CA 1985, s. 117 Where a company is originally incorporated as a public company it must, before doing any business or borrowing any money, obtain a certificate from the registrar of companies regarding minimum allotted share capital.

6.2.3 Old public companies

This applies to companies that should have re-registered as public companies or become private companies.

6.2.4 Non-commencement of business within one year of incorporation, or suspension of business for a whole year

The court will exercise its discretion to wind up the company provided it is sure that the company has no intention of carrying on business and is not likely to do so.

6.2.5 Membership below two persons

If the membership of a company falls below two persons the remaining member is liable (jointly and severally with the company) for debts of the company incurred after six months from the date when membership was reduced below two if the remaining member knows that there are no other members. In these circumstances a winding-up order is a means of avoiding that liability, but it is rare in practice. CA 1985, s. 24

6.2.6 Company unable to pay its debts

This is the most common ground for ordering a winding up. The Act provides for the circumstances in which a company is deemed to be unable to pay its debts:

(a) Where a creditor (whether as assignee or otherwise), whose debt is more than £750, has served a written demand at the company's registered office requiring the company to pay the debt and the company has for three weeks neglected to pay or secure the debt or offer a composition to the reasonable satisfaction of the creditor. s. 123(1)(a)

This demand, called 'the statutory demand', must state the amount of the debt, which must be presently payable. Interest, or other charges accruing from time to time, must be separately identified and limited to the amount accrued due at the date of the demand. The consideration for the debt must be set out (or, if none, the way in which the debt arises) in the demand. It must also contain an explanation of the purpose of the demand, the time-limits of, and methods of compliance with, the demand and a warning that non-compliance may result in winding-up proceedings against the company. The creditor must inform the company of the name, address and telephone number (if any) of named individual(s) with whom an officer or representative of the company can communicate with a view to securing or compounding for the debt. Finally, the statutory demand must be dated and signed by the creditor or his agent (which latter must certify his authority to act on the creditor's behalf). r. 4.4(2) r. 4.5(2) r. 4.5(1) r. 4.6(1) r. 4.6(2)

The Act requires that the statutory demand must be left at the company's registered office and this appears to preclude service of the demand by post. If the company does not have a registered office, service at its principal or usual place of business or at its unregistered office is permissible. The time-limit of 21 days may be extended by the court.

r. 4.3

s. 123(1)(b) (b) Where in England and Wales, execution or process issued on a judgment decree or order of any court in the creditor's favour is returned wholly or partly unsatisfied.

s. 123(1)(c) (c) Where, in Scotland, the induciae of a charge for payment on an extract decree, or an extract registered bond, or an extract registered protest, have expired without payment being made.

s. 123(1)(d) (d) Where, in Northern Ireland, a certificate of unenforceability has been granted in respect of a judgment against the company.

s. 123(1)(e) (e) Where it is proved to the satisfaction of the court that the company is unable to pay its debts as they fall due. It was stated in *Re Tweeds Garages Ltd* [1962] Ch 406 that 'a company may at the same time be insolvent and wealthy. It may have wealth locked up in investments not presently realisable; but although this may be so, yet if it have not assets available to meet its current liabilities it is commercially insolvent and may be wound up'.

Examples of inability to pay debts as they fall due are the dishonouring of a bill of exchange; statement of the company's solicitor to judgment creditor that there were no assets upon which to levy execution; and the fact that a company can meet some of its present obligations only by defaulting on others.

s. 123(2) (f) Where it is proved to the satisfaction of the court that the value of the company's assets is less than the amount of its liabilities taking into account its contingent and prospective liabilities.

Commercially this is the most worrying ground for assessing inability to pay debts, since if assets are to be valued on a break-up basis and undiscounted contingent debts based on guarantees, leases or warranty claims are taken into account many otherwise viable companies would be 'unable to pay their debts'. The commercial realities of such company trading ought to be taken into account by the court in employing what is basically a balance sheet method of assessing solvency, with the result that an unduly, and artificially, pessimistic approach to values should not be adopted as the basis of making a winding-up order.

6.2.7 'Just and equitable' grounds

The words 'just and equitable grounds' allow the court a wide discretion and they are not to be restricted by other grounds set out in s. 122. Accordingly, the court has used these grounds for winding up where:

(a) The substratum of the company has gone, for example, the loss of the entire property which the company was formed to acquire and exploit, such as confiscation of its oilfields (*Re Baku Consolidated Oilfields Ltd* [1944] 1 All ER 24). If the court is prepared to find that there is some overriding set of objects which the company was formed to pursue and which it cannot pursue, then the court will wind it up so that an investment in one kind of business company by a shareholder cannot be converted into an investment in a totally dissimilar kind of enterprise.

(b) The business of the company has been entirely finished (*Re Zinotty Properties Ltd* [1984] 1 WLR 1249).

(c) There is deadlock in the management so that it is impossible for the company to run its business (*Re American Pioneer Leather Co. Ltd* [1918] 1 Ch 556).

(d) The company is formed for illegal or fraudulent purposes (*Princess of Reuss* v *Bos* (1871) LR 5 HL 176).

(e) There is oppression of the minority by the majority in running the company's affairs.

6.3 Persons who may petition

In practice, the majority of winding-up petitions are presented by creditors. They are not, however, the only persons with the power to present a petition. The company, its directors or its contributories (wider in scope than just the existing members) may petition. The Secretary of State may ask for winding up, as may the official receiver, the company's administrator, administrative receiver or the supervisor of a voluntary arrangement. The grounds upon which the foregoing persons may proceed to ask for an order differ.

6.3.1 Creditors' right to petition

A creditor may petition on any ground under s. 122(1) but generally, the petition is based on the inability of the company to pay its debts. Under s. 123 (definition of inability to pay debts) only non-compliance with the statutory demand refers to a sum of money (currently £750). The other circumstances set out in s. 123 contain no reference to any financial limits. The sum of £750 will, however, generally be regarded as the minimum amount upon which a creditor's petition can be based (two or more creditors can join together to reach £750), but the court may order a winding-up where the debt is less than this amount if there appears to be no other way for the creditor to recover his debt (*Re World Industrial Bank Ltd* [1909] WN 148).

An assignee of a creditor is a creditor for the purposes of

petitioning. A contingent or prospective creditor petitioning on inability to pay debts can only invoke s. 123(1)(e) (company unable to pay its debts as they fall due) or s. 123(2) (value of company's assets is less than the amount of its liabilities, contingent and prospective liabilities being taken into account). The reason that he cannot petition under s. 123(1)(a) (statutory demand) is that if his debt is contingent or prospective it is not 'then due' (i.e., presently payable) at the date of serving the statutory demand. Equally such creditors cannot issue execution or other means of enforcement and are unable, therefore, to rely upon s. 123(1)(b) (unsatisfied executions etc.).

6.3.2 Petition by the company

s. 124(1) The company has power to present a petition against itself. This raises the question of who can authorise the company to present it. Prior to the Act the rule was that shareholders could, by ordinary resolution, decide that the company should petition and directors could not so authorise (*Smith* v *Duke of Manchester* (1883) 24 ChD
s. 124(1) 611). This appears still to be the law. There is statutory provision for the directors to present a petition themselves, but this is not the same as a provision to empower the directors to decide that the company shall do it. The point is not without significance because of the matter of costs. Further, a board resolution to authorise the company to petition, if it were possible, might in suitable circumstances be open to attack by minority shareholders, whereas if the directors petitioned personally, their statutory *locus standi* would not be liable to be similarly challenged.

6.3.3 The directors

s. 124(1) The directors can present a petition in their capacity as directors. Presumably this means by resolution of the board rather than by unanimous action. If a simple majority will suffice for such a decision to be made (as it would under most company articles) any dissenters should consider their position carefully. Neither the Act nor the Rules appear to give dissenting directors, as such, the right to appear in opposition to the petition of the board. The court should allow them to appear in these circumstances, since, if there is a difference of opinion, that is a material factor to be taken into account by the court when exercising its discretion under s. 125.

6.3.4 Contributories

s. 74(1) 'Contributory' means, subject to the qualifications listed below, any present or past member who is liable to contribute to the assets of the company in his character as member in respect of the company's debts, liabilities, liquidation expenses and adjustment of rights among contributories (even if the contribution is nil, e.g., because the shares are fully paid, a member is still a contributory). The qualifications on the general rule are as follows:

(i) anyone ceasing to be a member more than a year before the commencement of liquidation is not a contributory; s. 74(2)

(ii) past members are not liable for company debts or liabilities incurred after their membership ceased;

(iii) past members are not liable to contribute unless existing members cannot meet their contributions;

(iv) contributions on shares are limited to paying the unpaid amount of the share;

(v) in guarantee companies the limit is the amount of the guarantee. s. 74(3)

In order to be entitled to petition, a contributory must have held his shares for six out of the 18 months before winding-up commenced. This rule does not apply where the ground of winding-up is reduction of membership below two. s. 124(2)

Where a company has used its capital in order to effect either a redemption of its redeemable shares or a purchase of its own shares under CA 1985, Part V, and has commenced winding-up within a year of using such capital, any member whose shares were redeemed or purchased is liable, up to the extent of capital so paid to him, to contribute to the assets and, as such contributory, may petition for winding-up only under s. 123(1)(f) (inability to pay debts) and s. 123(1)(g) (just and equitable). A director who signed the declaration of solvency under CA 1985, s.173(3), without reasonable grounds for his opinion is a contributory for the purposes of this rule. Where a director has unlimited liability as director under CA 1985, ss. 306 and 307, he is a contributory (except in respect of debts incurred after termination of office) unless he vacated office more than a year before the commencement of liquidation. s. 124(3) and s. 76; s. 124(3) and s. 75

The court has imposed a condition on the right of contributories to petition, namely that they must have an 'interest' in the winding-up proceedings, i.e., either an expectation of a return of assets or a liability to make a contribution which may be called up by a liquidator (*Re Othery Construction Ltd* [1966] 1 WLR 69).

6.3.5 The Secretary of State

The Secretary of State may petition on the grounds only: s. 124(4)

(a) that the company is an 'old public company'; or

(b) that being originally incorporated as a public company it has not within a year of registration obtained a certificate entitling it to do business or borrow money; or

(c) that following an inspectors' report or from information obtained under an order for production of documents under CA 1985, ss. 447 or 448, he is of the opinion that it is expedient in the public interest to wind up the company if the court is of the view that it is just and equitable to do so.

6.3.6 The official receiver

s. 124(5) The official receiver may only present a petition for compulsory liquidation where a company is already in voluntary liquidation. He must satisfy the court that the voluntary liquidation cannot continue with due regard to creditors' or contributories' interests.

r. 10.2 The official receiver can, with the court's leave, authorise someone to act on his behalf. In emergencies, where there is no official receiver capable of acting, the registrar of the court may act. The powers of r. 10.2(b) delegation are said to apply 'in respect of any application to the court'.

6.3.7 Office holders

An administrator may petition for a winding-up order. He will, however, have to apply for the administration order to be set aside under s. 18 because a winding-up order cannot be made while an s. 11(3)(a) administration order is in force.

An administrative receiver and a supervisor of a voluntary arrangement may also petition for winding-up.

6.4 Procedure for presenting a petition

6.4.1 Courts to which petition may be presented

s. 117(1) The High Court may wind up any company registered in England s. 117(2) and Wales, and the Court of Session may wind up any company registered in Scotland. Such county courts as are designated by the Lord Chancellor may wind up companies whose paid-up, or credited as paid-up, share capital does not exceed £120,000 in whose district the registered office is (or failing such, the last known office or s. 118 principal place of business). Where proceedings are commenced in the wrong court, the court may either transfer them to the right court or retain the proceedings.

6.4.2 The petition

The following rules apply where the petitioner is other than a contributory:

(a) The petition must be filed in court and be verified by affidavit. r. 4.7(1)

(b) A receipt for the required deposit must be produced to the court. r. 4.7(2)

(c) There shall be delivered to the court with the petition:

(i) a copy exhibited to the affidavit of service; r. 4.7(3)(b)

(ii) a copy for service on the company (where the company is not the petitioner); r. 4.7(3)(a)

(iii) a copy each for service upon any voluntary liquidator, administrative receiver, supervisor and, in the case of banks and licensed institutions, the Bank of England. r. 4.7(4)

The court must seal the copies and state the venue for hearing the petition (venue means date, place and time of proceedings). r. 13.6

(d) The petition must be served on the company. Service should be personal as far as possible at the registered office (or, failing such, the last known registered office, or, failing that, the last known principal place of business) handed to a person declaring himself to be or believed to be a director, officer or employee or to a person acknowledging himself to be authorised to accept service. If there is no such person at the registered office, the petition may be left at the office. Failing that, court directions must be sought. Oversea companies are to be served in accordance with CA 1985, s. 695. r. 4.8 r. 4.8(5)

(e) An affidavit of service must be filed in court immediately after service with a sealed copy of petition or court order as to substituted service. r. 4.9

(f) Persons entitled to copies (see (c) above) must be served by dispatch of them on the business day following service of the petition on the company. r. 4.10

(g) The petition must be advertised in the *Gazette* unless the court otherwise directs. An advertisement should be made between seven days after the service of the petition and seven days before the hearing and must give the name and address (registered office or otherwise, as appropriate) of the company and of the petitioner (and of his solicitor if any), date of presentation of petition, venue for hearing, and a statement that those who wish to appear should give notice to that effect. r. 4.11

(h) At least five days before the hearing, the petitioner or his solicitor must certify (and give the details of) due presentation of service, advertising and date of hearing. A copy of the advertisement is to be filed with this certificate. The court can dismiss the petition for failure to comply with these rules. r. 4.14

(i) Anyone intending to appear on the petition must give notice r. 4.16

to do so by 4 p.m. on the business day before the hearing giving his name, address, telephone number (and similar details of anyone authorised to act for him), his intention to support or oppose the petition, and the amount and nature of his debt. (Late notices need
r. 4.18(1) court approval.) If the company intends to oppose the petition, it must file an affidavit of its opposition at least seven days before the
r. 4.18(2) hearing (sending a copy forthwith to the petitioner after it has been filed).

r. 4.17 (j) The petitioner must prepare for the court a list of the appearances before the commencement of the hearing giving details of relevant names and addresses (including respective solicitors) and whether they intend to support or oppose.

r. 4.15 (k) Withdrawal of a petition is possible up to five days before the hearing if there has been no advertisement, no notices to appear and if the company consents. The court's power is discretionary and the parties' costs are a matter of agreement.

Parties who cannot take advantage of rule 4.15 often commit a technical breach of other rules in order to have their petitions dismissed, but under rule 4.19 other persons, contributories or creditors, may be substituted by the court (a creditor may be substituted for a contributory: *Re Creative Handbook Ltd* (1984) 128 SJ 645).

r. 4.22 Where the petitioner is a contributory he must specify the grounds of his petition and file it in court with one copy for service on the company. The court then fixes a date for hearing (the return day) before the registrar (or as the court orders), states the return day upon the copy, seals it and returns it to the petitioner for service upon the company. Service must be made at least 14 days before the return day.

r. 4.23 On the return day, or afterwards, the court shall give such directions as it thinks fit for service, venue, particulars of claim or defence, advertisement, evidence, copies, or other matters.

With necessary modifications, the rules about notices and lists of appearances in (i) and (j) above apply.

6.5 Consequences of presenting a petition

6.5.1 Disposition of property may be invalid

s. 127 Any disposition of company property after the presentation of a petition is void unless approved by the court. In most cases, transactions entered into in the normal course of trade and completed before the winding-up order will be approved, but where the company has merely contracted to do something, and not completed it, it will not be approved. If the company pays a creditor after the presentation of a petition the court will not make that payment valid as to do so would go against the principle that creditors are to be ranked *pari passu*. The court has wide discretion in deciding which transactions it will validate and will generally uphold all proper transactions. The discretion is essential to avoid complete cessation of a company's trading, especially if the petition does not result in a winding-up order being made.

6.5.2 Status of members may not be changed

Any alteration in the status of members or transfer of shares is invalid unless approved by the court. A strong case is needed and proof of some benefit to the company should be shown in order to persuade the court to approve the transactions, unless the transfer was presented to the company before the company commenced winding-up and the directors have delayed. s. 127

6.5.3 Stay of proceedings

Before the court has made a winding-up order, a petition has the effect of staying any pending action or proceedings unless the court approves. (There is a similar restriction after the winding-up order is made.) s. 126(1)

6.5.4 Provisional liquidator

At any time after presentation of the petition and before the winding-up order is made any persons entitled to petition for winding-up may apply for the appointment of the official receiver or some other person as provisional liquidator. Affidavit evidence must be lodged setting out the grounds, consent of nominee (if not the official receiver), whether the company is in voluntary liquidation, subject to administration, or undertaking a voluntary arrangement, value of assets; and whether or not the official receiver has been notified. A deposit must accompany the application and the court's powers are discretionary. s. 135 r. 4.25

If the court appoints a provisional liquidator sealed copies of the order of appointment must be sent to the company, any liquidator, the official receiver or administrative receiver. *Ex parte* applications may result in undertakings in damages. The provisional liquidator has such powers as the court gives to him. Security may be required where someone other than the official receiver is appointed. r. 4.26 s. 135(4)

Remuneration (fixed by the court from time to time) and expenses are a charge on company property (and if a winding-up order is made are payable in the statutory order of priority) and may be paid out of the deposit if other funds are insufficient. A provisional liquidator may require a statement of affairs to be prepared. r. 4.30 r. 4.32

6.6 The winding-up order and its consequences

6.6.1 The court's powers

s. 125(1) The court treats a petition as a class action and not as a means of debt enforcement. The vital rule is that the court's powers are entirely discretionary when deciding whether or not to allow the petition. The factors that may affect the court's decision include:

(a) the wishes of other creditors or contributories;
(b) the existence of a bona fide dispute as to the debt on which a creditor's petition is based;
(c) whether the Rules have been complied with: since the volume of business in the companies court is considerable, procedural errors often lead to dismissal of the petition;
(d) if the petitioner is abusing the process of the court;
(e) unreasonableness of a contributory in refusing alternative relief under CA 1985, s. 459;
(f) existence of assets or prospects of assets (though s. 125 says that a petition should not be refused because there are either no assets or assets are charged beyond their value);
(g) whether the petitioner wishes to withdraw before advertisement;
(h) whether other creditors or contributories wish to carry on the petition after the petitioner has withdrawn or applied to have his petition struck out;
(i) possibility of advantages accruing to the petitioner which are not available to other creditors or contributories.

6.6.2 Consequences of the winding-up order

s. 130(4) Where the court makes a winding-up order the order operates in favour of every creditor and contributory. Three sealed copies are
r. 4.21 sent forthwith to the official receiver who sends one to the registrar of
s. 130(1) companies and one to the company. The official receiver must gazette the order and advertise it in a local newspaper.

s. 129 Compulsory liquidation is deemed to have commenced at the time of the presentation of the petition for winding up. If, however, the company was in voluntary liquidation prior to presentation of the petition the liquidation is deemed to have commenced at the time that the company passed the resolution to go into liquidation.

The immediate consequences of the making of a winding-up order are as follows:

s. 136(2) (a) the official receiver becomes liquidator except where, following an administration or a voluntary arrangement, the court appoints the administrator or supervisor to be liquidator; s. 140

(b) all actions and proceedings against the company must be stayed unless the court allows them to commence or continue on terms laid down by the court; s. 130(2)

(c) the official receiver, in any case where a winding-up order has been made, may require a statement of affairs to be made out (see 7.3); s. 131

(d) first meetings of creditors and contributories must be convened, unless dispensed with under s. 136(5), and a liquidation committee appointed if required; s. 141

(e) the directors' duties and powers cease;

(f) the business of the company can be carried on only so far as it is beneficial to the liquidation but it requires court sanction. sch. 4

6.7 Liquidators

The nature of the office of a liquidator in a compulsory liquidation is uncertain. The view that the liquidator is an officer of the court is given credence by rule 4.179 which states that the liquidator discharges his duties 'as an officer of the court subject to its control'. Certainly, when he exercises the powers expressly delegated to him under s. 160 (holding and conducting meetings, making calls etc.) he does so as an officer of the court. It is also possible to construe that in some circumstances a compulsory liquidator is an agent of the company, as in the case of schedule 4 to the Act, which empowers the liquidator to execute deeds, receipts and other documents 'in the name and on behalf of the company'.

6.7.1 Liquidator's appointment

The official receiver, by virtue of his office, becomes the liquidator of the company on the making of a winding-up order and continues in office until or unless another person becomes liquidator (see below). As indicated above, the only exception to this rule is that where a winding-up order is made immediately upon the discharge of an administration order or at a time when there is a voluntary arrangement in force the court may appoint the ex-administrator or the supervisor of the voluntary arrangement to be liquidator. At any time that a vacancy arises, the official receiver, again by virtue of his office, becomes liquidator. s. 136(2) s. 136(3)

The official receiver has 12 weeks from the winding-up order to decide whether or not to call first meetings of creditors and contributories to choose a liquidator in his stead. The Act introduces a discretion whereby the official receiver, if he considers that the holding of meetings will be of no benefit to the creditors or s. 136(5) contributories or that the cost of calling such meetings is unwarranted in relation to the available assets, may dispense with the meetings. He must, however, notify the court, the creditors and the contributories of this decision within the 12-week period. The creditors may compel him to hold a meeting if 25% in value so decides.

Where the official receiver decides to summon first meetings of creditors and contributories the following rules apply:

r. 4.50 (a) The meetings must be held within four months after the winding-up order.

r. 4.50 (b) Notice must be given to the court forthwith and to every known creditor and contributory respectively 21 days before the meetings and must specify a date not more than four days before the meetings by which proofs and (if applicable) proxies must be lodged for voting entitlement.

(c) Proxy forms must be sent with every notice and notice of the meetings must be advertised.

r. 4.52 (d) At the first meetings the only resolutions that may be passed are those relating to the appointment of a named insolvency practitioner to be liquidator (and if joint liquidators are appointed, whether or not they can act individually) and the appointment of a liquidation committee. At the creditors' meeting, if no liquidation committee is established, a resolution may be passed concerning the liquidator's remuneration and, if the meeting was requisitioned by the creditors, a resolution authorising payment of the cost of summoning and holding the meeting to be treated as a liquidation expense. If there are special reasons, the chairman may allow any other resolution.

r. 4.55 (e) The chairman will be the official receiver or a person nominated by him.

r. 4.100 (f) Where the meetings appoint someone other than the official receiver to be liquidator the chairman shall certify the appointment after the person has provided a written statement that he is an insolvency practitioner and that he is qualified to act as liquidator and consents to do so. The appointment is effective from the date on
r. 4.106 which the official receiver files a copy of the certificate in court, and must be advertised by the liquidator in a newspaper.

s. 139 (g) If the creditors' meeting and the contributories' meeting choose different people to be liquidator the creditors' choice prevails (subject to appeal to the court).

r. 4.102 Where an insolvency practitioner is appointed liquidator by the court following an administration or voluntary arrangement the appointment takes effect from the date of the court order. Unless the court allows him to advertise his appointment, the liquidator must give notice of it to all the known creditors and contributories and must state whether or not he intends calling meetings of creditors and contributories to appoint a liquidation committee.

The official receiver, in England and Wales, may apply to the Secretary of State for the appointment of some other person as liquidator in his place. If the application is granted the Secretary of State will specify the date from which the appointment is effective. Advertisement or notification by the liquidator follows the same rules as in the preceding paragraph. s. 137 r. 4.104

In Scotland, an interim liquidator is appointed when the winding-up order is made and he has 28 days within which to call a meeting of creditors (and of contributories if warranted) to choose him or some other person as liquidator. s. 138

6.7.2 Liquidator's powers and duties

The general duty of a liquidator or provisional liquidator is to take custody and control of all the property and things in action to which the company is or appears to be entitled, and he must ensure that the assets are got in, realised and distributed to the company's creditors and, if there is a surplus, to those entitled to such surplus.

In order to achieve these aims the liquidator may exercise powers specifically set out in the Act and detailed in chapter 7 (Rules common to all liquidations).

The duties of a liquidator include the following:

(a) He has a general duty to exercise his discretion in the management of assets and their distribution. This duty is personal and is not to be delegated (*Re Metropolitan Bank and Jones* (1876) 2 ChD 366). His power to appoint agents is to be exercised in relation to matters which he cannot do himself. There is, however, no restriction on the delegation of clerical or administrative tasks to his staff. Furthermore, the liquidator must not use his power to apply to the court under s. 145(1) as a means of avoiding the exercise of his discretion since the court will not do his job for him. Only in circumstances of genuine doubt or difficulty should the section be invoked. s. 168(4)

(b) Fiduciary duties—the liquidator is said to stand in a fiduciary relation to the company, its creditors and contributories. This is dealt with more fully in chapter 7 (Rules common to all liquidations).

(c) Co-operation with the official receiver—the liquidator, where he is not the official receiver, must give the information and s. 143(2) permit inspection of such books, documents and papers and give such other assistance as the official receiver may reasonably require.

s. 170 (d) Enforcement of duty to make returns etc.—the Act and the Rules provide many instances where a liquidator must file, deliver or make returns, accounts or other documents and serve notices. If he fails to comply, any creditor, contributory or the registrar of companies may apply to the court for an order requiring him to satisfy the requirements if, for at least 14 days after notice to comply, he has not obeyed. Costs fall on the liquidator.

s. 167(2) (e) Dispositions to a connected person—where the liquidator
s. 249 disposes of property to a person 'connected' with the company he must notify the liquidation committee. A person is 'connected' if he is a director, shadow director, 'associate' of such a person or if he is an 'associate' of the company. 'Associate' is defined in great detail in s. 435 of the Act but covers relatives, partners and employees and corporate association by virtue of common control (see 7.6.1);

(f) Duties applicable to all liquidators whether the company is being wound up voluntarily or compulsorily. These are dealt with in chapter 7 (Rules common to all liquidations).

r. 4.155 (g) Report all matters of concern to the liquidation committee.

s. 132 (h) The official receiver must investigate the causes of a company's failure and the promotion, formation, business, dealings and affairs of the company and report to the court if he thinks fit. If such a report is made it is *prima facie* evidence of the facts stated in it
s. 133 in any proceedings. He may apply to the court for a public examination of any person who has been concerned in the promotion, formation or management of the company or has acted as liquidator, administrator or receiver or manager, and, unless the court otherwise directs, he must apply on request by 50% in value of the creditors or 75% in value of the contributories.

r. 4.43 (i) The official receiver shall, at least once after the making of the winding-up order, send a report to creditors and contributories with respect to the proceedings in the liquidation and the state of the company's affairs. Where a statement of affairs (see 7.3) has been submitted and filed he must send a summary of the statement, and any observations he may make, to the creditors and contributories unless he has already sent a report and there is nothing further to add following submission of the statement. The court can
r. 4.47 relieve the official receiver of this duty if it thinks fit on consideration of the cost involved, the assets available and the extent of the interest of the creditors or contributories.

6.8 The liquidation committee

In a winding-up in England and Wales there is no liquidation committee when the official receiver is liquidator, the functions of such a committee being vested in the Secretary of State. In Scotland, if there is no liquidation committee, the functions are vested in the court. s. 141 s. 142

Where a company is being wound up on grounds that include the inability to pay its debts the first meeting of creditors may establish a liquidation committee comprising at least three and no more than five creditors; in a winding-up when the inability to pay its debts is not one of the grounds the contributories may, in addition, appoint up to three members. A liquidator must convene meetings for this purpose if one tenth in value of the creditors request it. If the creditors do not resolve to establish such a committee and the contributories do so resolve, the latter may apply for an order of the court directing a creditors' meeting to reconsider. If a committee is still not established the contributories alone may establish it with from three to five contributories as the members. r. 4.152 r. 4.154 s. 141(3) r. 4.154

Creditors who have proved their unsecured debts are eligible (corporate creditors acting by representative under rule 4.159) to be a member of the committee. A person cannot be both a creditor and a contributory member. r. 4.152

The liquidator issues a certificate (filed in court) of due constitution (which establishes the existence of the committee) when he has the agreement of three chosen members to serve on the committee. The liquidator must notify the court of any changes in the membership. Meetings of the committee are held when and where determined by the liquidator, the first meeting being called within three months of his appointment or the establishment of the committee, whichever is the later. A committee member may request the liquidator to call a meeting which the liquidator must do within 21 days. r. 4.153 r. 4.156

6.8.1 Functions

The functions of the committee are:

(a) To approve the making of a call by the liquidator.

(b) To authorise the carrying on of the company's business for the beneficial winding up.

(c) To agree to the payment of any class of creditors in full.

(d) To sanction any compromise or arrangement with creditors (or contributories where there is liability) and matters affecting assets and take security for debts and liabilities.

(e) To authorise the liquidator to bring or defend legal proceedings.

r. 4.155(1) (f) To receive liquidators' reports on matters of concern.

r. 4.155(2) (g) To request information.

r. 4.155(3) (h) If the committee was constituted more than 28 days after the appointment of a liquidator, to receive a summary report of his actions.

r. 4.168 (i) To demand reports (not more than once every two months) of the general progress of the winding-up. Failing this demand, reports be sent to the committee every six months.

r. 4.127 (j) To approve the basis of the liquidator's remuneration. (Where the official receiver is liquidator his remuneration is laid down in regulations.)

6.8.2 Procedures

The procedures relating to the meetings of the committee are as follows:

r. 4.156(3) (a) Seven days' notice of venue (unless waived) is required or as resolved by the previous meeting.

r. 4.157 (b) The chairman is the liquidator or his nominee (qualified or experienced).

r. 4.158 (c) A quorum is at least two creditor members following notice of the meeting to all. Members may appoint representatives (who attend with a letter of authority) who cannot be corporate bodies, undischarged bankrupts, debtors subject to compositions or arrangements, representatives of another member at the same time, or another member acting as such at the time.

r. 4.165 (d) Resolutions are carried by a majority of creditor members' votes (contributory members' votes do not count, unless creditors have been paid in full, in which case the creditor members of the
r. 4.171 committee vacate office and the liquidator certifies the position to the court). Resolutions may also be carried by post (notice being sent
r. 4.167 by the liquidator to all members containing a copy of the resolution; any committee member can, within seven days, demand a meeting).

r. 4.169 (e) Reasonable travelling costs are allowable as an expense of the liquidation.

6.8.3 Cessation of membership

A person ceases to be a member upon:

r. 4.160 (a) resignation;

r. 4.161 (b) bankruptcy (but trustee replaces him), composition or arrangement with creditors;

(c) absence for three consecutive meetings unless on the third occasion the committee waives this rule; r. 4.161

(d) cessation of status as creditor (or if found not to be such); r. 4.161

(e) removal by the appropriate meeting of creditors or contributories. r. 4.162

Vacancies need not be filled (provided the minimum number is still in office) if the liquidator and a majority of the remaining creditor members agree. Filling the vacancy is ultimately for majority decision by creditors or contributories as appropriate. r. 4.163 r. 4.163 r. 4.164

6.8.4 *Fiduciary position of liquidation committee*

There are restrictions upon the right of certain persons who are (or were during the previous 12 months) committee members, or are committee members' representatives or are associates of committee members or committee members' representatives. Such persons cannot receive payment for services or goods supplied in the liquidation, or obtain profits or acquire assets from the estate unless there is: r. 4.170

(a) prior court approval; or

(b) an urgent case or a pre-liquidation contract, but subsequent court approval must be sought without undue delay; or

(c) prior liquidation committee approval (without the vote of any person who has a direct or indirect interest in the transaction).

Failure to comply with the above rules renders the transaction voidable or the interested party liable to account for profits (associates may escape if they had no reason to believe rule 4.170 was being broken).

6.8.5 *Winding up following immediately upon administration*

If a winding-up order is made immediately after the discharge of an administration order and the person who was the administrator becomes the liquidator a creditors' committee established in the administration continues in being as the liquidation committee (with the addition in solvent liquidations of contributory members). A certificate by the liquidator must be filed in court establishing the committee in the liquidation and any changes in its composition. The main body of rules applying to a liquidation committee then govern this committee. r. 4.173 to 4.178

6.8.6 *Creditors paid in full*

If the creditors are paid in full the liquidator must file a certificate in r. 4.171

court and the creditor members cease to be members of the committee. The committee continues in being until abolished by the contributories although at least three contributory members are needed (but during the 28 days following the certificate less than three contributories can exist as the liquidation committee but cannot act). Contributories by resolution can increase the membership up to five (or the liquidator can co-opt).

6.9 Control of the liquidation by the court

The powers of the court include the following:

s. 147 (a) The court can stay all proceedings in the winding up on such terms as it thinks fit (and may require a report from the official receiver). Application may be made by the official receiver, liquidator, creditor or contributory.

s. 148 (b) The court shall settle a list of contributories but need not do so where calls are not needed and no adjustment of rights is involved.

s. 149(1) (c) The court can order contributories to pay money due from them to the company whether or not a call has been made (orders are
s. 149(2) conclusive evidence as to liability (s. 152)). Set-off is permissible, in the case of unlimited companies, but not in respect of debts due to the
s. 149(3) contributory arising out of his membership. Set-off is permissible in any case where debts are paid in full with interest.

s. 150 (d) The court can make calls on contributories (allowing for deficiency of contribution from some contributories).

s. 151 (e) The court can order any money due from any person to be paid into the Bank of England rather than to the liquidator.

s. 153 (f) The court can settle dates for proving debts and exclude a non-proving creditor from the benefit of distribution.

s. 154 (g) The court shall adjust contributories' rights and distribute the surplus.

s. 155 (h) The court can permit inspection of books and papers by creditors and contributories.

s. 156 (i) The court can, where assets do not meet liabilities, make such order as it thinks just for the priority of winding-up expenses.

s. 158 (j) At any time before or after the winding-up order the court can cause the arrest of an absconding contributory and the seizing and control of his books, papers and movable property.

s. 160 (k) Powers of delegation (see 7.2).

Other controls available to the court are included in chapter 7 (Rules common to all liquidations).

6.10 Winding-up unregistered companies

Unregistered companies cannot be wound up voluntarily. The court may order the winding-up of any association or company other than a specially incorporated railway company or registered company under the Joint Stock Companies Acts or other companies legislation. The general rule is that such companies may be wound up using all the provisions of the Act and the Companies Act. This general rule is subject to the following exceptions: s. 221(4) s. 220(1) s. 221(1) and s. 229(1)

(a) If there is a principal place of business in Northern Ireland the company is not to be wound up under the Act unless it has a principal place of business in England and Wales and/or Scotland. s. 221(2)

(b) The grounds upon which a petition may be presented are:

(i) The company is dissolved, has ceased to carry on business or carries on its business only for the purpose of winding up its affairs; s. 221(5)(a)

(ii) That it is just and equitable. s. 221(5)(c)

(iii) That the company is unable to pay its debts. The company is deemed to be unable to pay its debts in the following circumstances: s. 221(5)(b)

(1) it cannot pay its debts as they fall due; s. 224(1)(d)

(2) the value of the assets is worth less than the liabilities (including contingent and prospective liabilities); s. 224(2)

(3) where in England and Wales any enforcement against a member (in that capacity), the company or its nominal defendant is returned unsatisfied; s. 224(1)(a)

(4) the company has failed to comply with a statutory demand (on a debt then due of £750 or more) within three weeks of serving the demand upon the company at its principal place of business or delivery to any secretary, director, manager, principal officer or as directed by the court; s. 222

(5) following a notice served on the company (or others as in (4) above) that an action is instituted against a member for a debt due from the member as such or the company and within three weeks the company has not paid, secured or compounded for the debt or stayed the action or indemnified the defendant for all costs, damages and expenses of such action against the member; s. 223

(6) granting in Northern Ireland of a certificate of unenforceability; s. 224(1)(c)

(7) expiry of certain Scottish inducae without payment; s. 224(1)(b)

s. 225 (c) An overseas company incorporated abroad ceasing to carry on the business which it carried on in Great Britain may be wound up under the Act even though under the foreign law governing its incorporation it is dissolved or otherwise ceases to exist.

s. 226 (d) A contributory is anyone who is liable:

(i) to pay, or contribute to, the company's debts or liabilities;
(ii) to pay, or contribute to, the expenses of liquidation;
(iii) to pay, or contribute to, liability for adjustment of members' rights;

s. 227 (e) The power of the court to stay or sist proceedings between petition and winding-up order against the company extends to
s. 228 actions and proceedings against a contributory. A similar extension applies to proceedings against a contributory after making a winding-up order.

s. 221(7) (f) In Scotland, an unregistered company may be wound up by the court if there is a floating charge over property comprised in the company's property and undertaking, and the court is satisfied that the security of the creditor entitled to the benefit of the floating charge is in jeopardy. For this purpose a creditor's security is deemed to be in jeopardy if the court is satisfied that events have occurred or are about to occur which render it unreasonable in the creditor's interests that the company should retain power to dispose of the property which is subject to the floating charge.

6.11 Vacation of office of liquidator

6.11.1 Resignation or removal of liquidator

s. 172 and (a) A liquidator may resign on the grounds of ill health, intent to
r. 4.108(3) cease practice as a qualified insolvency practitioner, conflict of interest or change of personal circumstances precluding or making continuation in office impracticable, or, where there are joint liquidators, on the ground that he and his co-liquidators consider it inexpedient that he should continue. He must call a creditors' meeting setting out in the notice his intent, the rules as to his release, and a summary of receipts and payments.

s. 172(5) (b) A liquidator vacates office on ceasing to be a qualified insolvency practitioner (notifying the official receiver who then notifies the Secretary of State and the court).

s. 172(4) (c) A liquidator appointed by the Secretary of State may be removed by the Secretary of State. Notice of the reasons must be
r. 4.123 given to the liquidator and official receiver and time for

representations must be afforded to the liquidator. Removal must be notified to the liquidator and the official receiver and filed in court.

(d) A liquidator vacates office upon giving notice to the court and the registrar of companies following the holding of the final meeting (notice to include the decisions of the meeting). s. 172(8)

(e) A liquidator may be removed from office by court order. An applicant may be required to make a deposit or give security for costs. The costs of the hearing are not an expense of the liquidation unless the court so orders. Following the applicant's *ex parte* hearing, 14 days' notice to the liquidator and official receiver of the venue for hearing the application must be given. s. 172(2) r. 4.119

(f) A liquidator may be removed by resolution of the creditors at any time where appointed by creditors or contributories or where the official receiver is acting as a replacement after a vacation of office by someone else, or where appointed by the court either following an administration or after approving the nominee or nominees of the creditors' and/or contributories' meetings. In any other case a creditors' meeting can replace the official receiver, the court's appointee or the Secretary of State's appointee only if the meeting is held at the discretion of the court, or with the consent of the liquidator or at the request of one quarter in value of the creditors. s. 172(2) s. 172(3)

(g) A provisional liquidator may be removed only by order of the court.

The removal is effective when the official receiver files the certificate of removal in court (a reconciliation of the liquidator's receipts and payments with the Secretary of State's account must first be certified by the Secretary of State). r. 4.116(2) r. 4.116(4)

On vacation he must deliver up all property, books, documents and proofs to any successor. r. 4.138

6.11.2 Release of the liquidator

(a) Release on resignation or removal—release is effective once notice has been filed in court. s. 174(4)(a)

(b) Release on completion of liquidation—28 days' notice of the creditors' final meeting must be given to all proving creditors together with one month's notice in the Gazette. If at this meeting no resolution against release is made the liquidator will (after putting to the meeting his report, summary of receipts and payments and reconciliation, upon which he may be questioned) be released upon filing notice in court. If there is such a resolution, application must be made to the Secretary of State. s. 174 r. 4.125 s. 172(8)

(c) Release of the official receiver—where the official receiver s. 174(2) has been replaced other than by the court, release occurs when notice of replacement is filed in court and where replaced by the court, the court settles the time of the official receiver's release.

s. 174(3) If, when he is liquidator, the official receiver notifies the Secretary of State that for practical purposes his administration is complete the Secretary of State settles his release. In Scotland, this is determined by the Accountant of Court.

Chapter 7

Rules Common to all Liquidations

Chapters 5 and 6 dealt with the special features of the law that apply in compulsory, members' voluntary or creditors' voluntary liquidations but there are some fundamental features common to all types of liquidation. These include the immediate consequences of the commencement of liquidation, certain matters relating to administration and management, rules designed to see that all relevant information is extracted, and rules for the distribution of the estate. The assets available to a liquidator can be increased by certain provisions of the Act and there are some common powers to redress or punish misbehaviour.

This chapter is set out under the following headings:

7.1 Matters arising at the onset of liquidation

(a) Liquidators (other than the official receiver) must be qualified insolvency practitioners. There may be more than one appointed and their terms of appointment must specify whether their powers are joint or joint and several. s. 230 s. 231

(b) Liquidators are to be described by the style of 'liquidator' of the company rather than by name. s. 163

(c) Liquidators may forfeit remuneration if they solicit office. s. 164

(d) The acts of liquidators are to be valid notwithstanding any defect in appointment, nomination or qualifications. s. 232

s. 109 (e) The registrar of companies must be notified of the
r. 4.106 appointment of a liquidator.
s. 188 (f) All invoices, orders for goods or business letters must state that the company is in liquidation.

s. 148 (g) Whilst the court has power to rectify the register of members to ensure that those who are truly contributories are identified, no further share dealing or changes in membership will generally be permitted (though this is not to say that the courts cannot sanction such a course).

(h) The directors' powers to manage the business and deal with its assets cease as from the commencement of the liquidation.

s. 177 (i) A special manager may be appointed by the court on the
r. 4.206 application of the liquidator or provisional liquidator where the
to 210 nature of the company's business or the interests of the company's creditors, contributories or members generally require someone other than the liquidator to manage it.

7.2 Powers of a liquidator

sch. 4, The following powers may be exercised in a compulsory liquidation
pt I with the sanction of the court, in a creditors' voluntary liquidation with the sanction of the court or the creditors' committee or a meeting of creditors, and in a members' voluntary liquidation with the sanction of an extraordinary resolution:

(a) pay any class of creditors in full;
(b) make any compromise or arrangement with creditors;
(c) compromise any debt;
(d) compromise any question relating to the assets or the liquidation;
(e) take security in respect of (c) and (d).

sch. 4 The following powers may be exercised with sanction in a
pt II compulsory liquidation and without sanction in any voluntary liquidation:

(a) bring or defend any action or other legal proceeding in the name and on behalf of the company;
(b) carry on the business of the company so far as may be necessary for its beneficial winding-up.

sch. 4 The following powers may be exercised by any liquidator without
pt III sanction:

(a) sell any assets privately or by public auction;

(b) do all acts and execute all deeds, receipts and other documents using the company's seal if necessary;

(c) prove, rank, claim and receive dividends in the insolvency of any contributory;

(d) draw, accept, make or endorse bills of exchange or promissory notes on the company's behalf;

(e) raise money on security;

(f) take out in his official name letters of administration to deceased contributories;

(g) appoint agents to do any business he cannot do;

(h) do all other things necessary for the liquidation of the company's affairs and distribution of its assets.

Liquidators may exercise the power of the court to hold meetings s. 160
of creditors or contributories (and must do so in a compulsory s. 168
liquidation in England and Wales if requested in writing to do so by one tenth in value of either the creditors or contributories), to settle lists of contributories, and to make calls. In Scotland, if there is no s. 169
liquidation committee, the court may make an order that the liquidator may bring or defend actions and carry on business without the sanction of the court, and in a compulsory liquidation in Scotland the liquidator has the same powers as a trustee of a bankrupt estate.

Liquidators have wide powers in relation to seeking out assets and obtaining information about the company:

(a) The liquidator may apply to the court for an examination of s. 236
any officer or person known or suspected of having company property or of being indebted to the company or any person whom the court thinks capable of giving information concerning the promotion, formation, business, dealings, affairs or property of the company. The evidence may be used against the person giving it. s. 433
Under this section (which is also applicable to an administrator, administrative receiver, provisional liquidator and the official receiver) the court has power to arrest any person who fails to appear before it or who has absconded, or is about to abscond, and power to seize books, records and assets in that person's possession.

(b) There are duties to attend upon the liquidator as reasonably s. 235
required and to provide information on any matters affecting the promotion, formation, business, dealings, affairs or property of the company placed upon past or present officers, employees (including under a contract for services) and those who within one year before the appointment of a provisional liquidator or the commencement of

liquidation were either concerned in the formation of the company, were employees (including under a contract for services) or were officers or employees of a company which latter was an officer of the company in liquidation. In a compulsory liquidation this duty is also placed on any administrators, administrative receivers or liquidators.

s. 234 (c) A wide power exists for the court to order delivery of property, books, papers or records to the liquidator.

s. 246 (d) Any lien (other than one on documents of title held as security) on books, papers or records of the company is unenforceable.

(e) If it will assist the liquidator to carry out his duties he may search the land registration register (Land Registration Act 1925, s. 112AA).

7.3 Statement of affairs

A statement of affairs is required in a creditors' voluntary liquidation and may be required by the official receiver in a compulsory liquidation. In a members' voluntary liquidation a declaration of solvency is prepared, obviating the need for a further statement of affairs.

s. 99 In a creditors' voluntary liquidation the statement is prepared by the directors and laid before the first meeting of creditors. In a compulsory liquidation where the official receiver requires a statement to be prepared it must be prepared within 21 days, or
s. 131 longer if the official receiver allows, by such of the following as the official receiver may require:

(a) past or present officers;

(b) employees currently or within a year before the winding-up order who can give information;

(c) officers and employees (currently or within a year before the winding-up order) of a company which is or within that year was, an officer of the company in liquidation (employees includes those with a contract for services);

(d) those who took part in the company's formation within that year.

A statement of affairs must be made out on the standard forms, be
s. 99 verified by affidavit and show details of the company's assets and
s. 131 liabilities; the names and addresses of the company's creditors; the securities held by them respectively and the dates when the securities were given; and (in compulsory liquidation) such other information as the official receiver may require.

The cost of preparing the statement of affairs is an expense of the liquidation. In compulsory liquidation the official receiver files a copy of the statement in court, and in voluntary liquidation the liquidator delivers a copy to the registrar of companies within seven days of his appointment. The official receiver may apply to the court to limit disclosure of the contents of the statement if it would avoid prejudicing the liquidation but no such specific option is open in a voluntary liquidation although there is provision for the court's directions to be sought on any matter.

r. 4.33

r. 4.34

r. 4.35

7.4 Conduct of the liquidation

7.4.1 The keeping of books

The liquidator must keep minutes of the proceedings of, and records of every resolution of, any creditors' or contributories' meetings and of meetings of the liquidation committee. He must note any other matters necessary to give an accurate record of his administration. Separate financial records of receipts and payments must be kept. Where trade continues, a separate trading account must be kept and weekly totals of receipts must be recorded.

IReg, reg. 8

IReg, reg. 9

IReg, reg. 10

Accounts must be submitted to the Secretary of State every 12 months (within 30 days of such year end). At the end of the first year the accounts must be accompanied by a summary of the statement of affairs and explanations given of any reason for not disposing of assets referred to in the statement of affairs. Similar accounts (within 14 days) must be submitted to the Secretary of State on vacating office. Creditors and contributories are entitled (on request) to free copies of the accounts. The books may be audited by order of the Secretary of State who may require vouchers and information and may require inspection on demand of the liquidator's accounts, books and records.

IReg, reg. 12

IReg, regs 12 & 30

7.4.2 Bank accounts

In a compulsory liquidation, moneys received are to be paid into the Insolvency Services Account at the Bank of England (unless a local account is authorised) within 14 days (forthwith if the sum is £5,000 or more). In a voluntary liquidation, the liquidator may operate a bank account. However, funds must be paid into the Insolvency Services Account every six months unless a sum to be retained is certified as necessary for the immediate purposes of the liquidation.

IReg, reg. 4

Payments out of the account are made upon application to the Secretary of State or Department of Trade and Industry in compulsory and voluntary cases respectively.

IReg, regs 5 & 25

7.4.3 Management of the business

s. 233 Hitherto, certain monopoly suppliers of utility services have been able to insist on the payment of outstanding accounts due by the company before they would allow a supply to the office holder. This is now illegal under the Act but the supplier is entitled to require a personal guarantee from the liquidator or provisional liquidator in respect of future supplies. The supplies are:

(a) a public supply of gas;
(b) a supply of electricity by an electricity board;
(c) a supply of water by statutory water undertakers;
(d) a supply of telecommunication services by a public telecommunications operator.

s. 186 The court may rescind any contract made with the company and if any damages are payable they may be proved for in the liquidation.
r. 4.206 to 210 If a special manager is appointed the court settles the terms of appointment and may insist on security (which the special manager must maintain). Quarterly accounting periods apply. The termination of office arises if no winding-up order is made or if the court on application so decides.

7.4.4 Control of the liquidator's conduct

s. 195 The court may direct meetings of creditors and contributories to be held to ascertain their wishes. Application may be made to the court
s. 112 by the liquidator or any creditor or any contributory to order the conduct of the liquidation and determine all questions in the
s. 168(5) liquidation. In compulsory liquidations any person aggrieved by a decision of the liquidator may apply to the court.

s. 212 Action may be taken against a liquidator who has misapplied or misappropriated any assets of the company or is guilty of any misfeasance or breach of fiduciary or other duty (see 7.7.2 and 8.12).

The accounting and auditing of records and accounts has been
s. 192 referred to in the previous section. Additionally the liquidator in a
r. 4.223 voluntary liquidation must send reports on the state of the liquidation to the registrar of companies at the end of the first 12 months of the liquidation and six-monthly thereafter.

7.5 Assets in the liquidation

One of the differences between bankruptcy and liquidation is that in bankruptcy the trustee in bankruptcy succeeds to the bankrupt's property and becomes, by virtue of the Act, the owner of it, whereas in a liquidation the company's property does not vest in the liquidator unless he asks the court for an order transferring ownership of assets to him.

With statutory modifications all property belonging to the company at the commencement of liquidation, and after-acquired property, is available to satisfy the creditors' claims. Indeed, the creditors are the persons with the real interest in the assets when liquidation commences.

Some property may not be available because the contract for its acquisition specifies that in the event of liquidation (or insolvency) the company's interest in the property acquired will determine. Leases of land and goods (particularly capital equipment) frequently contain forfeiture clauses which will take the lease out of the assets available to the liquidator. If the company's equity in such property is substantial it may well be that an application for relief against forfeiture should be made (in practice all outstanding payments in respect of the property must be met as a normal condition of the court's relief). It may also happen that a liquidation or its conduct involves a breach of contract entitling the other party to determine the contract (*Sale Continuation Ltd* v *Austin Taylor & Co. Ltd* [1967] 2 All ER 1092).

7.5.1 Property held on trust

Property held by the company on trust is not available for distribution (*Barclays Bank Ltd* v *Quistclose Investments Ltd* [1970] AC 567, *Re Charge Card Services Ltd (No. 2)* [1986] 3 WLR 697). Where a trust instrument authorised a bank trustee to invest trust moneys with any banker, including itself, trust money held by it as a banker was not recoverable by the beneficiaries of the trust in priority to other creditors (*Space Investments Ltd* v *Canadian Imperial Bank of Commerce Trust Co. (Bahamas) Ltd* (1986) 1 WLR 27). Increasingly common nowadays are the setting up by companies of trust accounts to hold moneys of customers who have made advance payments in respect of goods ordered, which money is triggered out of the account only when the goods are supplied. Such arrangements are effective to enable customers to recover their advance payments as trust money if goods are not supplied (*Re Kayford Ltd* [1975] 1 WLR 279). If, however, such clauses operate to defeat the principle of *pari passu* distribution of a company's assets (*British Eagle International Air Lines Ltd* v *Compagnie Nationale Air France* [1975] 2 All ER 390) the clause will be struck down, see *Carreras Rothmans Ltd* v *Freeman Mathews Treasure Ltd* (1985) Ch 207.

7.5.2 Retention of title

Where a person has sold goods to the company under an effective retention of title clause the company will have no property in the goods. Many retention of title clauses have foundered as unregistered charges (*Re Bond Worth Ltd* [1980] Ch 228; *Borden (UK) Ltd* v *Scottish Timber Products Ltd* [1981] Ch 25; and *Re Peachdart Ltd* [1984] Ch 131) but in one of the more recent cases, *Clough Mill Ltd* v *Martin* decided in the Court of Appeal, ([1985] 1 WLR 111), it was decided that the intentions of the parties were of considerable importance and that although the whole clause might not be valid it was possible for the invalid part to be ignored and for the valid part to stand.

7.5.3 Incomplete executions and attachments

s. 183 Where an execution or attachment is not completed by a judgment creditor before liquidation commences the liquidator can prevent the enforcement from going through to completion and recover the assets (other than from a bona fide purchaser under any sheriff's sale).

An execution or attachment is complete in relation to goods by seizure and sale; a debt by receipt of the debt; and land by making a
s. 184 charging order under the Charging Orders Act 1979, s. 1. However, where a sheriff has sold goods in excess of £250 he must retain the proceeds for 14 days. If the sheriff receives notice that a winding-up petition has been presented or that a meeting of creditors has been called for the purpose of putting the company into liquidation, within the 14 days he must pay the proceeds, less his costs, to the liquidator.

In the case of voluntary liquidation, notice of the meeting at which it is proposed to wind up the company voluntarily is effective to prevent a judgment creditor who has such notice from being able to go ahead, thus embodying the principle in *Re Caribbean Products (Yam Importers) Ltd* [1966] Ch 331. The date of receiving such notice is effectively, therefore, substituted for the date of commencement of liquidation as far as the judgment creditor is concerned.

The above applies only in England and Wales. For a company registered in Scotland or for a company registered in England and Wales but with any estate in Scotland the provisions of s. 185 apply, dealing with the effect of sequestration on diligence and realisation of estate under the Bankruptcy (Scotland) Act 1985 suitably amended.

7.5.4 Unregistered charges

If a charge specified in CA 1985, s. 396, and created by a company in

England and Wales is not delivered to the registrar of companies within 21 days of the date of its creation it is void against the liquidator and any creditor of the company. (The court, however, in CA 1985, s. 404, may allow late registration if the omission was accidental or inadvertent, or if it would not prejudice the creditors or shareholders, or if it would be just and equitable.) Although the charge may become void this has no effect on any underlying contract and money secured by the charge becomes payable immediately. The charges, including mortgages, specified in s. 396 are:

(a) a charge for the purpose of securing any issue of debentures;
(b) a charge on uncalled share capital of the company;
(c) a charge created or evidenced by an instrument which, if executed by an individual, would require registration as a bill of sale;
(d) a charge on land (wherever situated) or any interest in it, but not including a charge for any rent or other periodical sum issuing out of the land;
(e) a charge on book debts of the company;
(f) a floating charge on the company's undertaking or property;
(g) a charge on calls made but not paid;
(h) a charge on a ship or aircraft, or any share in a ship;
(i) a charge on goodwill, on a patent or a licence under a patent, on a trade mark or on a copyright or a licence under a copyright.

7.5.5 Disclaimer

The power to disclaim onerous property applies only to a company in liquidation in England and Wales. A disclaimer operates to determine the rights, interests and liabilities of the company in or in respect of the property disclaimed but does not, except as far as is necessary for the purpose of releasing the company from any liability, affect the rights or liabilities of any other person. Despite having taken possession or endeavouring to sell or otherwise exercise rights of ownership in respect of any property the liquidator may still disclaim onerous property which, for the purpose of the Act is defined as any unprofitable contract and any other property of the company which is unsaleable or not readily saleable or is such that it may give rise to a liability to pay money or perform any other onerous act. [s. 178] [s. 178(3)]

Property cannot be disclaimed if a person interested in it has applied in writing to the liquidator for a decision on whether or not he will disclaim and no disclaimer notice has been given by the liquidator within 28 days of the date of the application. Any person sustaining loss following disclaimer may prove in the liquidation. [s. 178(5)]

7.6 Pre-liquidation (and pre-administration) transactions

Certain transactions prior to liquidation may be void or subject to challenge as a result of liquidation. As referred to in 3.8.6 in the chapter on administration orders a number of matters are common to both liquidators and administrators and both office holders have powers and duties to investigate the following matters (unless otherwise stated, these matters relate only to England and Wales).

7.6.1 Transactions at an undervalue and preferences

s. 238 A transaction at an undervalue is one by which the company made a gift, or transfer of property, for no consideration or for consideration significantly less in value than that provided by the company. Unless there were reasonable grounds for believing that the transaction would benefit the company and the transaction was entered into bona fide and for carrying on the business the liquidator or administrator may upset it if it occurred at a relevant time (defined below).

s. 239 A preference arises where a company puts one of its creditors, or a surety or a guarantor, into a position which, in the event of the company going into insolvent liquidation, will be better than the position he or it would have been in and may be upset by the liquidator or administrator if it occurred at a relevant time (defined below). However, the court will not make an order unless it can be shown that the desire to give preference influenced the company's decision to do so, and in the case of a preference to a connected person this is presumed unless proved otherwise.

s. 240 A relevant time is a time when the company was unable to pay its debts (as defined in s. 123) or became unable to pay its debts as a result of the transaction, and is within certain periods before either the company goes into liquidation or a petition for an administration order is presented, as follows:

(a) a preference (not at undervalue)—six months, but extended to two years when given to a connected person (other than an employee); and

(b) a transaction at undervalue—two years (in this case, where the transaction was with a connected person the company is assumed to be insolvent unless proved to the contrary).

s. 249 A person is connected with a company if he is a director or shadow director of the company or an associate of such a director or shadow
s. 435 director or is an associate of the company. An associate is defined at great length in the Act and encompasses almost any kind of relative

of an individual or his spouse. It also includes a person with whom he is in partnership and the relatives of that person, his employer or employees, and certain trustees, and a director or officer of a company is treated as being an employee. A company is an associate of another company if the same person has control of both companies, or if a person has control of one company and an associate has control of the other or if there is an associate relationship between groups of people controlling each company. A company is an associate of a person if that person has control of it.

Where a transaction at an undervalue, or a preference, has been given at a relevant time the liquidator or administrator may apply to the court for an order to restore the position to what it would have been if the company had not entered into the transaction. The court, if it makes an order, may require the return to the company of s. 241
property or money involved in the transaction, release or discharge of security given by the company, money to be paid in respect of benefits received, restoration of obligations under any surety or guarantee released by the company, provide for security to be provided or provide for the extent to which a person or company may prove in the liquidation. The court may make an order affecting any person, whether involved in the subject transaction or a subsequent transaction involving the same property, but will not prejudice a person who acquired the property in good faith and without notice of the relevant circumstances.

The Act incorporates similar provisions applicable in Scotland by virtue of s. 242, gratuitous alienations, and s. 243, unfair preferences. In addition to a liquidator or an administrator, a challenge may be made by any creditor where the company has gone into s. 242
liquidation. In respect of gratuitous alienations the relevant time is five years before the liquidation or administration order where the person is an associate of the company within the meaning of the Bankruptcy (Scotland) Act 1985, or two years in the case of any other person. Allowance is made for birthday, Christmas or charitable gifts to fall outside the scope of alienation. In respect of a preference s. 243
in favour of creditors to the prejudice of the general body of creditors the relevant time is six months before liquidation or the making of the administration order.

7.6.2 Extortionate credit transactions

The court may set aside all or part of a transaction, or vary its terms s. 244
or require payment or surrender of property, if the terms of it were such as to require grossly exhorbitant payments in respect of the provision of credit or if it otherwise grossly contravened ordinary

principles of fair dealing and if it was entered into in the three years before liquidation or the making of an administration order.

7.6.3 Avoidance of floating charges

s. 245 A floating charge on the company's property or undertaking created at a relevant time prior to liquidation or administration is invalid unless new moneys or fresh assets or services are received by the company by way of consideration at the same time as or after creation of the charge, or a debt is discharged or reduced. The relevant time is two years in the case of a charge given to a connected person, and 12 months in any other case, before liquidation or before the date of presentation of the petition for the administration order, and in either case between the presentation of a petition for making an administration order and the making of the order. Connected person is defined in 7.6.1. If the charge is in favour of a person not connected with the company it will not be invalid if the company, at the time it gave the charge, was able to pay its debts within the meaning of s. 123 and did not become unable to pay its debts as a result of the transaction. The provisions relating to the avoidance of floating charges apply in Scotland as well as England and Wales.

The courts, under the predecessor provision in the Companies Act 1948, s. 322, insisted that transactions should have been entered into bona fide for the company's benefit. It is not clear whether the interpretation of s. 322 of that Act by the Court of Appeal in *Mace Builders (Glasgow) Ltd* v *Lunn* [1986] Ch 459 will apply to s. 245. The Court of Appeal decided in that case that if a floating charge was made within the 12-month period and a receiver was appointed and the assets sold before liquidation commenced, the liquidator could not invalidate the charge. The Court of Appeal noted the opening words of s. 322 of the 1948 Act: 'Where a company is being wound up, a floating charge', and concluded that the section only invalidated charges still outstanding and unsatisfied at the time of liquidation. Section 245 does not carry the same opening words as s. 322 of the 1948 Act and it is possible that a future court decision may reach a different conclusion.

7.6.4 Unenforceability of liens

A lien or other right to retain possession of any books, papers or other records of the company is unenforceable against a liquidator, provisional liquidator or administrator except where documents give title to property and are held as such.

7.7 Malpractices before and during liquidation

7.7.1 Fraudulent trading

Any person who is knowingly a party to the carrying on of the company's business with intent to defraud its creditors, or with intent to defraud the creditors of any person, or for any fraudulent purpose, can be made to contribute to the company's assets following application to the court by the liquidator. s. 213

The test is one of dishonesty (*Re Patrick & Lyon Ltd* [1933] Ch 786) and there is no difference between 'dishonesty' in the commercial context and 'dishonesty' in any other context (*R* v *Lockwood* [1986] Crim LR 244 CA). Examples of dishonesty include taking an unjustified 'risk' to the 'detriment or prejudice' of another (*R* v *Sinclair* (1968) 52 Cr App R 618); and incurring a debt without any reasonable expectation that it will be paid (*Re William C. Leitch Bros Ltd* [1932] 2 Ch 71; *R* v *Grantham* [1984] QB 675).

Fraudulent trading, so far as it relates to directors, and wrongful trading, which relates entirely to past or present directors, are dealt with in 8.9.

7.7.2 Misfeasance proceedings

Where any person who is or was concerned or participated in the promotion, formation or management of a company, is or was an officer of it or has been liquidator, administrative receiver or administrator of it, has misapplied, retained, become liable or accountable for any of the company's money or property or has been guilty of misfeasance, or breach of fiduciary or other duty to the company, then such person may be made liable therefor. Application to the court may be made by the official receiver or the liquidator, or any creditor or contributory (with the leave of the court) for repayment, restoration or account or compensation against the delinquent. s. 212 s. 212(3)

The reference to breach of 'fiduciary or other duty' in relation to the company changes the orthodox view of the predecessor section in the Companies Act 1948, s. 333, that negligence was not actionable under the section as far as directors were concerned. This view was based on *Re B. Johnson & Co. (Builders) Ltd* [1955] Ch 634. Oddly, negligence was an actionable breach of duty under s. 333 as against liquidators and creditors.

Where directors commit a breach of duty which would be actionable under s. 212, they cannot be pursued under s. 212 if the breach has been effectively ratified by the shareholders (*Multinational Gas & Petrochemical Co.* v *Multinational Gas & Petrochemical Services Ltd* [1983] Ch 258; and see the reasoning of

Slade LJ in *Rolled Steel Products (Holdings) Ltd* v *British Steel Corporation* (1986) Ch 246).

7.7.3 Improper dealings

s. 206 to 210 Officers of the company are guilty of an offence if they have dealt improperly and with fraudulent intent with the company's assets or records, or if they made material omissions from the statement of affairs or fail to make full disclosure concerning property and records to the liquidator.

7.7.4 Investigation of malpractice

s. 218(1) and (2) Apart from the usual channels of investigation by police authorities, the court (in a compulsory liquidation) can, on the application of any interested person or of its own motion, direct the matter to be handed over to the prosecuting authorities (the power to conduct a public or private examination may be a source of acquiring information). If it appears to the liquidator that offences have been committed by past or present officers or that any member is guilty of an offence he shall report it to the official receiver.

s. 218(3) to (6) In the case of voluntary liquidations the liquidator may report offences by past or present officers or any member to the prosecuting authority furnishing and giving access to relevant information (he may be compelled to refer a matter to the prosecuting authority where the court so orders on the application of any interested person or of its own motion). The prosecuting authority may refer the matter to the Secretary of State for further enquiry (the Secretary of State is vested with the powers of inspectors appointed under CA
s. 219(1), (2) 1985, s. 431 or 432). The Secretary of State may demand information and answers to questions put by him may be used in evidence. The liquidator, officers and agents of the company (past or present) other
s. 219(3) than the defendants must give all assistance where criminal proceedings are instituted.

7.8 Application of assets

The general rule is that costs and expenses of the liquidation are paid first and then the creditors receive payment of their debts (and interest) and any surplus belongs to the contributories. The rules for the order of payment of costs and expenses and the agreement and priority of creditors' claims are set out below.

7.8.1 Order of payment of costs and expenses

r. 4.218 The costs and expenses in a liquidation are payable out of the assets in the following order:

(a) expenses properly chargeable or incurred by the official receiver or the liquidator in preserving, realising or getting in any of the assets of the company;

(b) any other expenses incurred or disbursements made by the official receiver or under his authority, including those incurred or made in carrying on the business of the company;

(c) (i) fees payable for the performance by the official receiver of his general duties as official receiver;

(ii) any repayable deposit lodged by the petitioner as security for the above fees;

(d) any other fees payable to the official receiver, and any remuneration payable to him under general regulations;

(e) the cost of any security provided by a provisional liquidator, liquidator or special manager;

(f) the remuneration of the provisional liquidator (if any);

(g) any deposit lodged on an application for the appointment of a provisional liquidator;

(h) the costs of the petitioner, and of any person appearing on the petition whose costs are allowed by the court;

(i) the remuneration of the special manager (if any);

(j) any amount payable to a person employed or authorised to assist in the preparation of a statement of affairs or of accounts;

(k) any allowance made, by order of the court, towards costs on an application for release from the obligation to submit a statement of affairs, or for an extension of time for submitting such a statement;

(l) any necessary disbursements by the liquidator in the course of his administration (including any expenses incurred by members of the liquidation committee or their representatives and allowed by the liquidator, but not including any payment of capital gains tax in circumstances referred to in (o) below);

(m) the remuneration or emoluments of any person who has been employed by the liquidator to perform any services for the company;

(n) the remuneration of the liquidator, up to any amount not exceeding that which is payable to the official receiver under general regulations;

(o) the amount of any capital gains tax on chargeable gains accruing on the realisation of any asset of the company (without regard to whether the realisation is effected by the liquidator, a secured creditor, or a receiver or manager appointed to deal with a security);

(p) the balance, after payment of sums due under paragraph (n) above, of any remuneration due to the liquidator.

7.8.2 Agreement of creditors' claims

In any liquidation, before the liquidator can distribute the funds arising from the company's assets in the order set out in 7.8.3 below, he must agree the quantum of the creditors' claims, unless, of course, there are no funds available to be distributed.

The procedure for agreeing claims in a compulsory liquidation is formal but in voluntary liquidations it is informal and the liquidator may use his discretion as to the extent to which he requires documentary evidence of claims. In a members' voluntary liquidation, where all creditors will be paid in full, the liquidator is unlikely to require any formal proof.

In a creditors' voluntary liquidation the liquidator is likely to require all creditors to confirm the amount of their claim but the requirement for further evidence will depend on the state of the company's books and the nature of the claim. Where a creditor
r. 4.73(3) claims (whether or not in writing) for his debt he is referred to as 'proving' and any document by which he seeks to establish his claim
r. 4.82 is his 'proof'. A claim may be admitted in whole or in part but if the liquidator rejects part of a claim he must give his reasons to the creditor in writing. An aggrieved creditor may apply to the court for a reversal or variation of the liquidator's decision. A proof may be withdrawn or varied at any time by agreement between the creditor and the liquidator.

r. 4.73 In a compulsory liquidation anyone claiming to be a creditor and wishing to recover his debt in whole or in part must submit a formal proof of debt. The required forms must be sent to the creditors by the liquidator with the first notice sent by the liquidator to the creditors. Full details of the creditor, the amount and details of his claim,
r. 4.75 whether or not the claim includes VAT or interest, whether the claim is preferential or secured and details of any documents that can substantiate the claim must be given in the proof.

The following rules apply to the quantification of creditors' claims:

r. 4.86 (a) The liquidator may estimate the value of contingent or unquantified claims.

r. 4.87 (b) The liquidator may reject a proof for money owed on a bill of exchange, promissory note, cheque or other negotiable instrument or security if the claimant cannot produce the original instrument or a certified copy.

r. 4.88 (c) A secured creditor may either realise his security and prove for any balance of his debt or may surrender his security and prove for the whole debt (any surplus realised by a secured creditor is payable to the liquidator). There are detailed rules for valuing security, surrendering it, redemption by the liquidator or testing its value. rr. 4.95 to 4.99

(d) All trade and other discounts, except any discount for immediate or cash settlement, must be deducted from a claim. r. 4.89

(e) Mutual dealings between a creditor and the company prior to liquidation must be set off. r. 4.90

(f) Debts in foreign currency must be converted to sterling using the Bank of England middle market rate for the day when the company went into liquidation. r. 4.91

(g) Debts of a periodic nature, such as rent, may be claimed up to the date of liquidation on an accruals basis. r. 4.92

(h) A debt payable at a future date may be proved but any dividend paid on such a debt is reduced to take account of early payment. r. 11.13

(i) A claim for an interest-bearing debt may include interest up to the date of liquidation. If interest has not been previously reserved or agreed it may be claimed if the debt is due by virtue of a written instrument and payable at a certain time but only from that time to the date of liquidation. In any other case interest can only be claimed if a written demand for payment was made prior to liquidation stating that interest would be payable from the date of demand to the date of payment, in which case interest can be claimed from the date of demand to the date of liquidation. The rate of interest may be subject to section 17 of the Judgments Act 1838. r. 4.93

(j) Dividends or other sums due to members of the company in their capacity as members do not rank with the claims of creditors but will rank as a claim on any surplus funds. s. 74(2)(f)

The following legal points relate to proofs of debt:

(a) Transactions which defeat the *pari passu* principle of distribution are of no effect. The Act cannot be contracted out of by parties (*British Eagle International Air Lines Ltd* v *Compagnie Nationale Air France* [1975] 1 WLR 758; *Carreras Rothmans Ltd* v *Freeman Mathews Treasure Ltd* [1985] Ch 207).

(b) The set-off rules where there are mutual debts, mutual credits or other mutual dealings between the company in liquidation and another cannot be ousted by contract (*Rolls Razor Ltd* v *Cox* [1967] 1 QB 552).

(c) Directors guilty of fraudulent trading or wrongful trading who are also creditors of the company may be ordered to rank for payment of their debts after all other debts (plus interest). s. 215(4)

(d) Two proofs cannot be submitted in respect of one debt, thus a guarantor cannot prove for the whole of his liability and the guaranteed creditor prove for the whole amount (*Re Oriental Commercial Bank* (1871) LR 7 Ch App 99; *Barclays Bank Ltd* v *TOSG Trust Fund Ltd* (1984) AC 626).

r. 12.3 (e) Provable debts include all claims present, future, certain or contingent, ascertained or sounding only in damages.

7.8.3 Priority and payment of claims

r. 4.180 A liquidator has a duty to declare and distribute dividends to creditors whenever he has sufficient funds to do so after providing for liquidation costs. Creditors who held security over specific assets will have either realised those assets in full or part satisfaction of their debts or, if the liquidator has realised the assets, will have been paid out of the proceeds. The funds available for distribution thereafter must be paid according to the following order of priority with each class of creditors being paid in full before any distribution can be made to the next class, and where there are insufficient funds to pay a class of creditors in full the claims must be abated in equal proportions:

s. 175 (a) *Preferential creditors.* The claims of preferential creditors are payable first out of any assets that are not subject to a floating charge. If such assets are insufficient to meet the claims in full, recourse is made to assets subject to a floating charge in priority to the holder of that floating charge.

The categories of preferential debts are listed below and are the same in liquidations, administrative receiverships, voluntary arrangements and individual insolvency. The relevant date in compulsory liquidations is the date of the winding-up order or the date of appointment of a provisional liquidator except where the liquidation follows on from the discharge of an administration order in which case the relevant date is the making of the administration order; in a voluntary liquidation it is the date of the resolution to put the company into liquidation; in receivership it is the date of the appointment of the administrative receiver in England and Wales or of the receiver in Scotland; in voluntary arrangements it is the date of the approval of the arrangement or, if an administration order is in force, the date of the order. The rules for individual insolvency are dealt with in 13.10.2.

The categories are:

(i) PAYE, and deductions made by the company in relation to subcontractors in the construction industry, deducted from emoluments paid in the 12 months prior to the relevant date;

(ii) VAT referable to the six months prior to the relevant date;

(iii) car tax due in the 12 months prior to the relevant date;

(iv) general betting duty, bingo duty or gaming licence duty due in the 12 months prior to the relevant date;

(v) National Insurance contributions due in the 12 months prior to the relevant date;

(vi) contributions to occupational pension schemes and State scheme premiums under schedule 3 to the Social Security Pensions Act 1975;

(vii) employees' remuneration due in the four months prior to the relevant date but not exceeding the sum prescribed by the Secretary of State, presently £800;

(viii) accrued holiday remuneration due to employees in respect of any period of employment before the relevant date;

(ix) advances by a third party for the payment of employees' emoluments or holiday remuneration that would, but for the payment, have fallen within (vii) or (viii) above.

(b) *Floating charge.* Where there is a floating charge that has not been crystallised by the appointment of an administrative receiver or by some other event, any funds realised from assets covered by the charge that are not required by the liquidator for the payment of preferential claims, will be payable to the holder of the charge in, or towards, satisfaction of his debt.

(c) *Unsecured creditors.* The claims of all creditors who are neither secured nor preferential and who have proved their debts rank equally amongst themselves. Where VAT bad debt relief has been claimed by the creditor his debt must be reduced by the amount of VAT. r. 4.181

(d) *Interest.* If all secured, preferential and unsecured creditors have been paid in full, including any creditors whose debts only become due after dividends have been paid (rule 11.13), any surplus funds then remaining become available for payment of interest on debts proved in the liquidation for the period since the liquidation commenced. Interest is payable, on all classes of debts, at the rate specified in the Judgments Act 1838 as amended from time to time (currently 15%) unless there is a higher rate of interest applicable to any particular debt. s. 189

(e) *Contributories.* Any surplus funds remaining after satisfaction in full of the liabilities in (a) to (d) above is distributable to the members of the company according to their rights and interests. s. 154

At any time that a liquidator intends to pay a dividend to any class of creditors he must give not less than 21 days' notice of that intention to any creditors of that class who have not proved their debts, specifying a date by when proofs must be lodged. Notice of the r. 11.2

actual dividend must then be given to all creditors who have proved
r. 11.6 their debts and the dividend payment may accompany that notice. The notice must give details of asset realisations, liquidator's payments, provisions for unsettled claims, the total amount distributed and the rate of dividend, and whether and when any further dividend is expected to be declared. If no dividend or no further dividend is to be declared the liquidator must notify creditors either that no funds have been realised or that the funds realised have already been defrayed or distributed.

r. 11.8 A creditor's proof may be increased or decreased at any time. If it is increased after a dividend has been paid he is entitled to be paid any arrears of dividend before any further dividend is paid to other creditors. If his proof is reduced after a dividend has been paid, the creditor must reimburse any overpayment to the liquidator.

7.9 Dissolution of the company

7.9.1 Early dissolution in compulsory liquidations

s. 202 In compulsory liquidations the official receiver (if liquidator) may apply to the registrar of companies for an 'early dissolution' of the company if it appears to him that the realisable assets do not cover his expenses and that the company's affairs do not require further
s. 202(3) investigation. He must first serve 28 days' notice upon the creditors,
s. 203 contributories and any administrative receiver of his intention. Any of these persons may apply to the Secretary of State to postpone the
s. 203(2) dissolution and an appeal lies to the court. The grounds of the application for postponement are that the expenses are covered by assets, or that the company's affairs do require further investigation or that there are other reasons that justify postponement.

If there are no applications for postponement, the official receiver
s. 202(4) is under no duty to act further in the liquidation and three months
s. 202(5) after the date when the registrar of companies registers the official receiver's application the company will be dissolved. This new
s. 204 provision is a useful means of saving expense. Similar provisions apply in Scotland.

7.9.2 Compulsory liquidations generally

s. 205 Where the registrar of companies receives a notice of the final creditors' meeting or a notice of completion of the liquidation from the official receiver he must register the notice and the company will be dissolved three months later unless the Secretary of State (subject to appeal to the court) defers dissolution on application by the official receiver or any interested person. Any deferment must be notified by a successful applicant to the registrar of companies within seven days of receipt of the decision of the Secretary of State or the court. rr. 4.224 and 225

7.9.3 Dissolution in voluntary liquidation

Where a final return and account has been filed with the registrar of companies by the liquidator under s. 94 or s. 106, the company is deemed to be dissolved three months after the registrar of companies has registered the return, unless the court, on application by the liquidator or other interested person, in its discretion decides to postpone dissolution. Within seven days after the court's decision a copy of the order of the court must be delivered to the registrar of companies. s. 201

7.9.4 Effects of dissolution

Property or rights vested in the company (other than as trustee) pass as *bona vacantia* to the Crown (or Duchy of Lancaster or Duchy of Cornwall) unless the court declares the dissolution void on application by a liquidator, or other person appearing to be interested within two years of the date of dissolution. The court may order the company to be restored to the register within 20 years of striking off following application by any person aggrieved. This ground for restoration to the register only applies where at the time of striking off the company was carrying on business, or was in operation, or if it is otherwise just that the company be restored. CA 1985, s. 654 CA 1985, s. 651 CA 1985, s. 653

Chapter 8

Insolvency and Directors

8.1 Introduction

Under the Companies Act 1985 and its predecessors a person could be disqualified from acting as a director on a number of grounds but the Insolvency Act 1985 introduced new provisions that extended the likelihood of disqualification of delinquent directors. As part of the consolidation of insolvency statutes the law on disqualification is now to be found in a single statute, the Company Directors Disqualification Act 1986 ('CDDA' 1986) and side-notes in this chapter are to that Act except where stated otherwise. The Act extends to England and Wales and to Scotland.

There are two broad areas of conduct that usually may, and in some circumstances must, result in a person being disqualified from being involved in the management of companies. The first broad area is general misconduct in connection with the promotion, management and liquidation of companies: this may be described as the pre-Insolvency Act 1985 provisions. The second area is unfitness to be a director: this arises predominantly out of the innovatory provisions of the Insolvency Act 1985.

8.2 The general power of the court to disqualify

s. 1(1) The effect of a disqualification order is to prohibit a person, without leave of the court, from:

(a) being a director of a company;
(b) being a liquidator or administrator of a company;
(c) being a receiver or manager of a company's property; or
(d) in any way, whether directly or indirectly, being concerned or taking part in the promotion, formation or management of a company.

In the event of such an order being made, it will run for a specified period beginning with the date of the order. Each section that
s. 1(2) provides for a disqualification order to be made specifies the

maximum (and in the case of unfit directors of insolvent companies, the minimum) period of disqualification that may (and in the case of unfit directors of insolvent companies must) be imposed. It is not s. 1(4)
necessary for the making of a disqualification order that the conduct on which it is based is criminal in nature, though, of course, this will often be the case. In the event of a disqualification order being made s. 1(3)
against a person who is already the subject of such an order, the periods specified in the order will run concurrently.

8.3 Disqualification on conviction of indictable offence

When a person is convicted of an indictable offence in connection s. 2(1)
with the promotion, formation, management or liquidation of a company or with the receivership or management of a company's property, the court may make a disqualification order against him. The key point here is conviction of an offence which may be tried on indictment and it is immaterial whether the trial was in fact on indictment or whether it took place summarily. In this context, the court that may make the order is: s. 2(2)

(a) any court that has jurisdiction to liquidate the company in relation to which the offence was committed;
(b) the court at which the person was convicted; or
(c) in the case of the person being summarily convicted, any other magistrates' court acting in the same petty sessions area.

The power of the court to make a disqualification order does not sch. 2
extend to anything done before 15 June 1982 by a person in his capacity as liquidator of a company or in the receivership or management of the property of a company. Likewise it does not extend, in the case of a summary conviction, where the person convicted has consented to be tried before 15 June 1982.

The maximum period of disqualification under this section is 15 s. 2(3)
years except where the order is made by a court of summary jurisdiction, in which case the upper limit is 5 years.

8.4 Disqualification for persistent breaches of companies legislation

A disqualification order may be made where it appears that a person s. 3(1)
has been persistently in breach of companies legislation requiring any account, return, notice or other document to be filed with, delivered or sent to the registrar of companies. Events prior to 1 June 1977 are disregarded. The maximum period for which disqualifi- s. 3(5)
cation may be ordered is five years. The meaning of 'persistent' is not defined, but, without prejudice to any other manner of proof, it is s. 3(2)
presumed that there has been a persistent failure if in the five years

ending with the date of the application the person has been adjudged guilty of three or more defaults of these filing requirements; the
s. 3(3) convictions may be on the same or different occasions, and either on indictment or summarily. Moreover, a person is 'adjudged guilty'
s. 3(3) not simply on conviction, but where a default order is made against him under any of the following provisions:

(a) CA 1985, s. 244 (order requiring delivery of company accounts);
(b) CA 1985, s. 713 (enforcement of company's duty to make returns);
(c) IA 1986, s. 41 (enforcement of receiver's or manager's duty to make returns);
(d) IA 1986, s. 170 (enforcement of liquidator's duty to make returns).

s. 3(4) In this context, the court that may make the order is any court that has jurisdiction to liquidate any of the companies in relation to which the offence or other default has been, or is alleged to have been, committed.

It would appear from two reported cases that the courts have tended towards leniency for what they perceived as a not particularly serious default. In *Re Civica Investments Ltd* [1983] BCLC 456, a director of a number of companies had been convicted on 48 occasions of defaults in relation to accounts and 11 in relation to annual returns, and an application for a disqualification order was made by the Secretary of State. The judge was influenced by the fact that some of the companies concerned were not trading, that there had been difficulties in preparing the accounts of two of the companies and that most of the defaults had been remedied by the date of the trial, and in the event a disqualification order was made for one year only. In *Re Arctic Engineering Ltd (No. 2)* [1986] 1 WLR 686 a liquidator had failed on 35 occasions to make returns to the registrar of companies, although he had never been prosecuted in respect of these matters, nor had there been made an enforcement order against him. It was held that the liquidator had been persistently in default under what is now CDDA 1986, s. 3, but a disqualification order was not made as the liquidator had not been dishonest, nor had he been incompetent, and an order would have had very serious consequences for the liquidator, his clients and his employees. Both the above cases were heard prior to the inception of the new legislation.

8.5 Disqualification for fraud

A disqualification order may be made where, in the course of the liquidation of a company, it appears that a person: s. 4(1)

(a) has been guilty of an offence for which he is liable under CA 1985, s. 458 (i.e., that he knowingly has been a party to the carrying on of the business of the company either with the intention of defrauding the company's creditors or the creditors of any other person, or for any other fraudulent purpose); or

(b) has otherwise been guilty, while an officer or liquidator of the company or receiver or manager of its property, of any fraud in relation to the company or of any breach of his duty as such officer, liquidator, receiver or manager.

In (a) it is expressly stated that it is irrelevant whether the person has been convicted or not. In (b) there is an exception in the case of anything done before 15 June 1982 by a person in his capacity as liquidator of a company or as receiver or manager of a company's property. Apart from this, s. 4 applies in relation to an offence committed or other thing done before 15 June 1982, though in respect of such a matter the maximum period for which a disqualification order may be made is five years. sch. 2

The court that may make a disqualification order under this section is any court having jurisdiction to liquidate any of the companies in relation to which the offence or other default has been, or is alleged to have been, committed. s. 4(2)

With the exception referred to, the maximum period of disqualification under this section is 15 years. s. 4(3)

8.6 Disqualification on summary conviction

Where a person is convicted of certain summary offences, the court by which he is convicted, or any other magistrates' court acting for the same petty sessions area, may make a disqualification order against him given that the following conditions are satisfied: s. 5(2)

(a) the conviction is for a summary offence committed after 14 June 1982; and s. 5(1) sch. 2

(b) the offence relates to a contravention of, or failure to comply with, any provision of the companies legislation requiring a return, account or other document to be filed with, delivered or sent, or notice of any matters to be given, to the registrar of companies, whether the contravention or failure is on such person's own part or on the part of the company; and s. 5(1)

(c) during the five years ending with the date of the conviction, s. 5(3) the person has had made against him, or has been convicted of, at least three defaults, orders and offences as detailed in (b).

s. 5(5) The maximum period for disqualification is five years. Events before 1 June 1977 are disregarded.

8.7 Disqualification for unfitness

s. 7(3) If it appears to a liquidator, an administrator, an administrative receiver or the official receiver that, in relation to a company with which he is dealing, a person is or has been a director or shadow director of the company which has become insolvent (either while he was a director or subsequently) and that the person's conduct as a director of that company, either considered in isolation or taken together with his conduct as a director of any other company, makes him unfit to be concerned with the management of a company, he
s. 7(1) must forthwith report the matter to the Secretary of State. If the Secretary of State is satisfied that it is expedient in the public interest that a disqualification order should be made, he may make an application to the court for the director to be disqualified. If the company is in compulsory liquidation, the Secretary of State may direct that the application shall be made by the official receiver.
s. 7(2) Except with the consent of the court, an application for a disqualification order may not be made after the end of a period of two years beginning on the day on which the company became insolvent.

s. 7(4) Insolvency practitioners have no duty to investigate the directors' conduct. Their duty is only to report on matters that have come to their attention in the course of their dealings with the company's affairs. Upon receiving the report, however, the Secretary of State or the official receiver may require the insolvency practitioner to provide him with such information with respect to any person's conduct as a director of the company and to produce and allow inspection of such books, papers and other records relevant to that person's conduct as director as the Secretary of State or the official receiver might reasonably require in reaching his decision whether to make an application for a disqualification order against that person.

s. 6(1) It is a prerequisite to the operation of this section that the company
s. 6(2) is insolvent, and the meaning of insolvent in this context is if:

(a) it goes into liquidation at a time when its assets are insufficient to pay its debts and other liabilities and the expenses of the winding up;
(b) an administration order is made against the company; or
(c) an administrative receiver of the company is appointed.

Given that the above criteria are satisfied, disqualification is mandatory and the court must make a disqualification order against the director. The minimum period is two years and the maximum is 15 years, but no application may be made under s. 6 where the company went into liquidation before 28 April 1986. s. 6(1) s. 19(c)

As stated above, the basis of the disqualification is the conduct of the directors. Conduct includes conduct in relation to any matter connected with or arising out of the insolvency of the company. In determining whether a person's conduct is such as to make him unfit to be a director, the court must have regard to factors outlined in schedule 1. The schedule is divided into two parts and the general matters to be considered by the court are: s. 6(1) s. 6(2) s. 9(1)

(a) Matters applicable in all cases: sch. 1

(i) any misfeasance or breach of any fiduciary or other duty by the director in relation to the company;
(ii) any misapplication or retention by the director of, or any conduct by the director giving rise to an obligation to account for, any money or other property of the company;
(iii) failure to comply with statutory requirements relating to books and records, returns and accounts.

(b) Matters applicable where the company has become insolvent:

(i) responsibility for the causes of the insolvency or for losses suffered by customers who made advance payments;
(ii) involvement in any transaction or preference that can be set aside;
(iii) failure to comply with statutory requirements relating to the insolvency.

The Secretary of State may modify any of the provisions of the schedule, so that the situation may arise in the future when the court will be applying the Secretary of State's criteria in deciding the Secretary of State's request that a person be disqualified as a director. s. 9(4)

Every liquidator, administrator, administrative receiver or the official receiver is required to submit a return to the Secretary of State within six months of his appointment, even if he has no knowledge of any conduct that would render any director unfit to be concerned in the management of a company. The detailed rules as to how the reports are made to the Secretary of State are provided by the Insolvent Companies (Reports on Conduct of Directors) No. 2 Rules 1986 (SI 1986 No. 2134) and the Companies (Disqualification Orders) Regulations (SI 1986 No. 2067). These set out standard forms which must contain certain basic information including the trade or profession of the director; the position he held within the company; his remuneration, expenses and benefits in kind over the previous three years; and details, where applicable, of the conduct of the director that make it appear that he is unfit to be a director. If a detailed report cannot be filed within six months of the office holder's appointment, an interim report must be filed within that period.

8.8 Disqualification after investigation of company

s. 8(1) When a report is made to the Secretary of State by inspectors appointed under CA 1985, s. 437, the Secretary of State may apply to the court for a disqualification order against any director or shadow director of the company in respect of which the investigation took place if he considers it expedient in the public interest to do so. The same power applies where the Secretary of State receives
s. 8(2) information or documents under CA 1985, ss. 447 or 448. The yardstick to be adopted by the court is whether the conduct of the director was such as to render him unfit to be concerned in the management of a company. The maximum period of disqualification
s. 8(4) under this provision is 15 years, but there is no specified minimum period. No application will be made in relation to a report made or information or documents obtained before 28 April 1986.

8.9 Disqualification for fraudulent or wrongful trading

The meanings of fraudulent trading (IA 1986, s. 213) and wrongful trading (IA 1986, s. 214) are discussed below, but broadly these provisions give the court power to declare that a person, in specified circumstances, should be personally liable to contribute to the assets
s. 10(1) of the company. A further sanction is that a court making a declaration that such a contribution should be made may also make a disqualification order. The maximum period of disqualification
s. 10(2) under this provision is 15 years but there is no specified minimum period.

8.9.1 Fraudulent trading

IA 1986, s. 213 If in the course of the liquidation of a company it appears that any business of a company had been carried on with intent to defraud creditors of the company or creditors of any other person, or for any fraudulent purpose, the liquidator may apply to the court for an order that any persons who were knowingly parties to the carrying on of the business in this way should make such contributions to the company's assets as the court thinks proper.

Although liquidators are unlikely to make much use of this

provision since the new concept of wrongful trading is likely to be easier to prove with a less burdensome standard of proof, there are three minor changes in the wording of the provision on fraudulent trading (as compared with CA 1985, s. 630) that should be noted:

(a) Proceedings can now be commenced only by the liquidator, whereas previously they could also be taken by a creditor.

(b) Any moneys ordered to be paid must go to the liquidator for the benefit of creditors generally, whereas previously the courts could order that payment should be made to a specified creditor.

(c) In the event of the person against whom proceedings in fraudulent trading are taken being himself a creditor of the company, the court may order that his debt should be postponed so as to rank after all other debts owed by the company.

8.9.2 Wrongful trading

If, in the course of a liquidation, the liquidator is satisfied that a director or shadow director is or has been guilty of wrongful trading, he may apply to the court for a declaration that such person is liable to make a contribution to the company's assets. The court must be satisfied on three criteria: IA 1986, s. 214(1)

(a) that the company has gone into insolvent liquidation (i.e., its assets are insufficient for the payment of its debts and other liabilities and the expenses of the liquidation); IA 1986, s. 214(6)

(b) that at some time before the commencement of the liquidation of the company, the director knew or ought to have concluded that there was no reasonable prospect that the company would avoid going into insolvent liquidation; and

(c) that he was a director of the company at the time.

A director will be taken to have known that the company could not avoid going into insolvent liquidation if that would have been the conclusion of a reasonably diligent person having both the general knowledge, skill and experience that might reasonably be expected of a person carrying out that particular director's duties with the company and the general knowledge, skill and experience actually possessed by that director. IA 1986, s. 214(4)

The court will not make an order under this section if it is satisfied that the director against whom the order is sought took every step with a view to minimising the potential loss to the company's creditors that he ought to have taken in the circumstances. IA 1986, s. 214(3)

8.9.3 Procedural rules common to both fraudulent and wrongful trading

Upon an application for either fraudulent or wrongful trading, the liquidator may himself give evidence or call witnesses. When the IA 1986, s. 215(1)

IA 1986, s. 215(2) court makes a declaration, it may give any further directions it feels necessary to give effect to the declaration. In particular it may provide that the liability of a director under the declaration shall be a charge on any debt owing by the company to him or on any charge on assets of the company held by him or any person on his behalf. From time to time the court may make such further order as may be necessary to enforce any charge so imposed.

IA 1986, s. 215(4) As has been mentioned above in the context of charges in fraudulent trading, the court may, in the event of the person against whom proceedings in fraudulent trading are taken being himself a creditor of the company, order that his debt should be postponed so as to rank after all other debts owed by the company. These IA 1986, s. 215(5) provisions apply notwithstanding that the director may be criminally liable for fraudulent trading.

8.10 Restriction on the use of company names

IA 1986, s. 216(1) Where a company goes into insolvent liquidation there are restrictions on the use that persons who were directors or shadow directors of the company at any time within the year before the company went into liquidation can make of the company's name. IA 1986, s. 216(2) The way in which the provision operates is that the name of the insolvent company, or any former name or trading name used during the year prior to liquidation, becomes a prohibited name, as does any name so similar as to suggest an association with the relevant IA 1986, s. 216(3) company. Persons who were directors or shadow directors in the circumstances outlined above must not, except with the leave of the court or in circumstances outlined below, during the five years after their company went into liquidation:

(a) be a director of any other company that is known by a prohibited name;

(b) be concerned or take part in any way in the promotion, formation or management of any such company; or

(c) be concerned or take part in the carrying on of a business in any way which is conducted under a prohibited name.

The circumstances in which a person to whom the statutory prohibition applies may act without leave of the court are:

IR 1986, r. 4.228 (a) When a successor company acquires the whole, or substantially the whole, of the business of an insolvent company from an insolvency practitioner (acting as liquidator, administrator or administrative receiver, or as supervisor of a voluntary arrangement) it may give notice to the insolvent company's creditors. The notice must be given within 28 days of the completion of the arrangements and must set out the names and trading names of both companies, and may name a person who has been a director or shadow director of the insolvent company (giving particulars of the nature and duration of that directorship) with a view to his being a director of the successor company or being otherwise associated with its management.

(b) Where that person makes an application to the court for leave to use a prohibited name within seven days of the company's going into liquidation and such leave is granted not more than six weeks from that date, he may use the prohibited name without committing an offence under IA 1986, s. 216. IR 1986, r. 4.229

(c) Where the company using the prohibited name has been known by that name for a period of one year ending with the day before the insolvent company went into liquidation and has not during that year been a dormant company within the meaning of CA 1985, s. 252(5). IR 1986, r. 4.230

In all other cases the leave of the court is required. When considering an application for leave, the court may require the liquidator, or any former liquidator, of the liquidating company to report on the circumstances in which the company became insolvent and to what degree the applicant was apparently responsible for its doing so. IR 1986, r. 4.227

Anyone who acts in breach of these provisions is guilty of a criminal offence. IA 1986, s. 216

8.11 Personal liability of persons acting while disqualified

The provisions concerning the disqualification of delinquent directors are strengthened by rules imposing personal liability upon those who act in contravention of a disqualification order. The persons concerned are those against whom a disqualification order has been made or who are banned from acting by virtue of being undischarged bankrupts but who nevertheless concern themselves in the management of a company, and also persons who act in the management of a company under instructions given by someone who is subject to a disqualification order or who is an undischarged bankrupt. Such persons become personally liable for all debts incurred by the company while they were involved in its management or willing to act on the instruction of disqualified persons. The liability for the debts of the company is joint and several with that of the company. s. 15(1) s. 15(2)

8.12 Personal liability of delinquent directors and others

If, in the course of a liquidation, it appears that any person who is or has been an officer of the company, or has acted as liquidator, IA 1986, s. 212(1)

administrator or administrative receiver of the company, or has
taken part in the promotion, formation or management of the
company, has retained or misapplied assets of the company, or been
guilty of breach of a fiduciary duty, proceedings may be taken
IA 1986, against him. The petitioner may be an official receiver, the liquidator
s. 212(3) or any creditor or contributory. The court may examine the conduct
of the respondent and compel him to repay any money he may have
taken or restore any assets to the company, or otherwise to
contribute such sum to the company's assets by way of compensation
for his breach of duty as the court thinks just. If the petitioner is a
IA 1986, contributory, he can make application only with the leave of the
s. 212(4) court. If the person against whom the order is sought is someone who
IA 1986, has acted as liquidator or administrator of the company and he has
s. 212(5) been released from his office, again proceedings can only be brought
with the leave of the court.

8.13 Undischarged bankrupts

s. 11(1) It is an offence for an undischarged bankrupt to act as a director of,
or directly or indirectly to take part in or be concerned in the
promotion, formation or management of, a company except with the
s. 11(3) leave of the court. Before such leave can be given, notice of the
intention to apply for it must be served on the official receiver whose
duty it is, should he believe that it would be contrary to the public
interest for leave to be given, to attend the hearing of the application
and oppose it.

8.14 Register of disqualification orders

s. 18(2) The Secretary of State must continue to maintain the register of
disqualification orders, and of cases in which leave has been granted
for a person subject to such an order to do anything which otherwise
s. 18(2) the order prohibits him from doing. This register was set up under
s. 18(1) CA 1976, s. 29, and continued under CA 1985, s. 301. The register is
maintained from information supplied to the Secretary of State by
officers of the courts. Regulations are contained in the Companies
(Disqualification Orders) Regulations 1986 (SI 1986 No. 2067). These
provide for a senior official at each court having jurisdiction to
disqualify to notify the Secretary of State by means of completion of
s. 18(1) a standard form. Notification has to be made to the Secretary of
State in cases when:

(a) a disqualification order is made;

(b) any action is taken by a court in consequence of which such an order is varied or ceases to be in force; or

(c) leave is granted by a court for a person subject to such an order to do anything which otherwise the order prohibits him from doing.

The register is open for inspection 'on such fee as may be specified by the Secretary of State in regulations', although at present no fee is payable. When an order of which entry is made in the register ceases to be in force, the Secretary of State must delete the entry from the register together with all particulars relating to it. s. 18(4) s. 18(3)

Chapter 9

Voluntary Arrangements in Individual Insolvency

9.1 Introduction

Both the Cork Committee (Cmnd 8558) and the White Paper, *A Revised Framework for Insolvency Law* (Cmnd 9175), stressed the need for a type of voluntary arrangement that could be used by individual debtors who wanted to come to terms with their creditors with the minimum of formality. Because deeds of arrangement bind only creditors who assent to them this method of settling financial difficulties fell into disuse, with the result that many individual debtors went bankrupt unnecessarily. The Act has introduced a new system, making it easier and safer for individuals to make binding arrangements with their creditors with the minimum of official involvement.

r. 5.1 The first stage of this procedure is for the debtor to formulate a proposal for a voluntary arrangement that he intends to put to his creditors.

s. 253(2) Under such a proposal, provision has to be made for an insolvency practitioner to act in relation to the composition or scheme, either as trustee or otherwise, for the purpose of supervising its implementation; this person is referred to as 'the nominee'.

s. 253(3) The proposal may be instigated by the debtor or, if the debtor is an undischarged bankrupt, by the debtor, the trustee of his estate or the official receiver, or may arise (where the debtor has already
s. 274(3) presented his own bankruptcy petition) as a result of the report made by an insolvency practitioner appointed by the court (see 10.2.4).

9.2 The proposal

s. 256(2) The debtor must prepare for the intended nominee a proposal setting out the proposed arrangement with an explanation of why it is believed that a voluntary arrangement is desirable and why creditors may be expected to agree with it. r. 5.3(1)

The proposal must contain details of the assets to be included in (or excluded from) the arrangement and assets to be provided by others, and the nature and amount of the debtor's liabilities. There must also be details as to how the liabilities are proposed to be met, modified, postponed or otherwise dealt with under the arrangement, with particular reference to the claims of preferential, secured and associated creditors. The proposal must also state whether, to the debtor's knowledge, there are any circumstances which give rise to the possibility, in the event of bankruptcy, of any claims relating to transactions at an undervalue, preferences or extortionate credit transactions, and if there are, what provision has been made to indemnify the estate in respect of such claims. r. 5.3(2) s. 339 s. 340 s. 343

Other information to be given in the proposal includes the nature of any guarantees given by other persons and the relationship of the guarantors with the debtor; the proposed duration of the voluntary arrangement and the proposed dates of distributions to the creditors, with estimates of the amounts; the amount to be paid to the nominee and supervisor of the arrangement by way of remuneration and expenses; details of the supervisor's functions and his qualifications; whether any person is offering guarantees for the purposes of the arrangement and, if so, whether any security is to be given or sought; the way in which funds held for the purpose of the arrangement are to be managed pending distribution; what is to be done with undistributed funds once the arrangement has ended; the way in which the debtor's business is to be conducted during the course of the arrangement; and finally details of any credit facilities that are to be arranged for the debtor and the way in which the debts arising thereunder are to be dealt with.

Formal notice of the proposal must be given to the intended nominee, and if that person agrees to act he must return a copy of the notice to the debtor endorsed with the date of receipt. If the debtor is an undischarged bankrupt, notice must also be given to the official receiver and the trustee, if there is one, specifying the name of the nominee. s. 253(4)

9.3 Application for an interim order

If an individual intends to proceed with a proposal to his creditors, application may be made to the court for an interim order. The application may be made by the debtor or, if he is an undischarged bankrupt, either by him, the trustee of his estate (if there is one) or the official receiver. s. 253(1) s. 253(3)

s. 253(5) An application for an interim order may not be made if a bankruptcy petition presented by the debtor is pending and the court has already appointed a qualified insolvency practitioner to prepare
s. 274(3) a report. However, upon the report being made the court may make an interim order without an application.

r. 5.5 The application must be accompanied by an affidavit confirming the basis of the application, and by the endorsed copy of the notice given to the intended nominee. A hearing date will be set by the court, and at least two days' notice of the hearing must be given to the nominee, any creditor who has presented a bankruptcy petition and, if applicable, the debtor himself, the official receiver and the trustee in bankruptcy.

s. 254 While an application for an interim order is pending, the court may stay any action, execution or other legal process against the property or person of the debtor. Proceedings pending against him in any court may be stayed or allowed to continue on such terms as that court thinks fit.

9.4 The interim order

s. 255(2) The court may make an interim order where it will assist the consideration and implementation of the debtor's proposals, and while the order is in force the nominee will submit a report to the court. The purpose of an interim order is to protect the debtor's property or, in the case of an undischarged bankrupt, to provide for the conduct of the bankruptcy pending consideration of the
s. 255(1) proposals. The court, however, may make an interim order only if it is satisfied that the debtor intends to make a proposal and that, on the day of making the application, he was an undischarged bankrupt or was in a position to be able to petition for his own bankruptcy. The debtor must not have made a previous application for an interim order during the 12 months ending with the day of the present application. The court must also be satisfied that the nominee is qualified to act as an insolvency practitioner and is willing to act in relation to the debtor's proposal.

s. 252(2) The effect of an interim order is that, while it is in force, no bankruptcy petition relating to the debtor may be presented or proceeded with and, unless the court gives leave, no other proceedings and no execution or other legal process may be
s. 255(3) commenced or continued against the debtor or his property. If the debtor is an undischarged bankrupt, an interim order may contain provision as to the conduct of the bankruptcy and the administration
s. 255(4) of the bankrupt's estate. The order may stay bankruptcy proceedings or modify the provisions of the Act or of the Rules in their

application to the debtor's insolvency. Such a modification will not be made in the interim order, however, unless the court is satisfied that it is likely to result in any significant diminution in, or in the value of, the debtor's estate for the purposes of the bankruptcy. s. 255(5)

If an interim order is made following an application it will cease to have effect at the end of the period of 14 days beginning with the day after the making of the order. s. 255(6)

The court will fix a time, before the order expires, for consideration of a report by the nominee. r. 5.6(3)

The court may extend the period for which the interim order has effect, either at the request of the nominee so as to enable him to have more time to prepare his report, or at the request of the debtor if the nominee has failed to submit the report required under this procedure. If the order is made under s. 274(3), it will cease to have effect at the end of such period as the court may specify as the period necessary to enable the creditors to consider the debtor's proposal. s. 256(4) s. 256(3) s. 274(4)

9.5 Procedure after an interim order has been made

When an interim order has been made, the nominee must submit a report to the court not less than two days before the order expires. The nominee will have received a copy of the proposal, and may also call upon the debtor for additional information. The debtor is required to produce a statement of affairs within seven days after his proposal is delivered to the nominee (or longer if the nominee allows), giving full details of assets and liabilities, although any statement produced in relation to pending bankruptcy proceedings may be used. r. 5.10 r. 5.9 r. 5.8

If the debtor fails to comply with these obligations the court may discharge the interim order. s. 256(6)

This information will enable the nominee to prepare his report to the court stating whether, in his opinion, a meeting of the debtor's creditors should be summoned to consider the debtor's proposals. If he considers that a meeting should be so summoned he must state the proposed date, time and place of such a meeting. The nominee must also submit his comments on the proposal and a copy or summary of the statement of affairs. The report is placed on the court file and may be inspected by any creditor. These documents must also be sent by the nominee to any creditor who has presented a bankruptcy petition and, if the debtor is an undischarged bankrupt, to the official receiver. If, following the nominee's report, the court is satisfied that a meeting of the creditors should be summoned to consider the debtor's proposals, the period of the interim order will be extended s. 256(1) r. 5.10 r. 5.13

to give sufficient time for the meeting to be held. In any event this must be between 14 and 28 days after the nominee submits his report.

s. 256(6) If for any reason, on application of the nominee, the court is satisfied that it would be inappropriate that a meeting of the creditors be summoned to consider the debtor's proposal, it may discharge the interim order.

s. 256(3) Where the nominee fails to submit the required report the court may, on the debtor's application, direct that the nominee be replaced as such by another insolvency practitioner and/or extend or, if it has expired, renew the interim order for such further period as the court may specify.

9.6 Consideration of the proposal

r. 5.13 If the nominee concludes in his report that a meeting of creditors should be summoned to consider the proposal, and the court does not direct otherwise, he must fix a date for the meeting to be held within 14 to 28 days of the filing of his report in the court. The notice must be sent at least 14 days before the meeting and must specify the court to which the nominee's report has been delivered and the rules relating to majorities at the meeting. The notice must be accompanied by a copy of the proposal, a copy or (if the nominee thinks fit) a summary of the statement of affairs, including a list of creditors, the nominee's comments on the proposal and a proxy form. The notice must be sent to all the creditors specified in the statement of affairs and any other creditors of whom the nominee is aware.

The purpose of the creditors' meeting is to decide whether to
r. 5.14 approve the proposals. The meeting must be held between 10 a.m. and 4 p.m. on a business day and the venue must be fixed to suit the convenience of the creditors. The meeting will be chaired by
r. 5.15 the nominee or by a nominated substitute, who must be either a qualified insolvency practitioner or an employee of the nominee, or
r. 5.17(4) his firm, who is experienced in insolvency matters. The chairman has the power to admit or reject all or any part of a creditor's claim for
s. 259 the purpose of his entitlement to vote. A report of the meeting must
r. 5.17(8) be made by the chairman to the court and, within 28 days of this
r. 5.17(5) report, the chairman's decision whether to accept or reject a claim may be appealed by any creditor or the debtor. If the court considers
r. 5.17(7) that what has happened gives rise to unfair prejudice or material irregularity it may order another meeting to be summoned or make
r. 5.17(6) such other order as it thinks fit. If the chairman is unsure whether to admit or reject a claim, he must mark it as objected to and allow the

creditor to vote. Should the objection to the claim later be upheld, the creditor's vote will be declared invalid.

Every creditor who has been given notice of the meeting is entitled to vote at the meeting or any adjournment of it. If a creditor fails to give the chairman written notice of his claim either before or at the meeting, however, his vote will not be counted. The vote will be calculated according to the amount of the creditor's debt, either at the date of the meeting or of an earlier bankruptcy order, although there is no voting right for unliquidated debts or for those whose value is unascertained unless the chairman estimates a minimum value for them. The votes of secured creditors will only be counted for the unsecured part of their claim for which the chairman has received written notice before or at the meeting. In these circumstances the chairman may exercise his discretion in allowing the vote to count. r. 5.17(1) r. 5.18(3) r. 5.17(2) r. 5.17(3) r. 5.18(3)

At the meeting a resolution to approve the proposal or any modification must be passed by a majority of three-quarters in value of creditors present, in person or by proxy, and voting. Other resolutions must be passed by a simple majority. A resolution, however, will be invalid if those who vote against it include over half in value of the 'creditors'. For this purpose, 'creditors' includes those to whom notice of the meeting was sent, whose votes have not been excluded by the chairman in accordance with r. 5.18(3) and who the chairman believes are not associates of the debtor. r. 5.18(1) r. 5.18(2) r. 5.18(4)

The chairman may hold a proxy vote but, unless otherwise directed by the proxy, he may not use this vote to vary the remuneration or expenses of the nominee or supervisor of the arrangement. If he does so, his vote with the proxy will not count towards the majority. r. 5.16 r. 5.18(6)

The meeting may be adjourned until the proposal is either accepted or rejected by creditors. If, on the day on which the meeting was summoned, the creditors do not approve the proposals, the chairman may adjourn for up to 14 days. Any final adjournment must be within 14 days of the original meeting and if the proposal is not agreed by then it is deemed to be rejected. r. 5.19(1) r. 5.19(2) r. 5.19(3)

The meeting may approve the proposed composition or scheme, or may approve it with modifications. The modifications may include replacing the proposed nominee with another person qualified to act as an insolvency practitioner. There can, however, be no modification which would result in the proposal falling outside the scope of the Act nor can any modification be approved unless the debtor consents to it. Furthermore, the meeting cannot approve any proposal or modification that affects the rights of any secured or preferential creditor to enforce its security or to receive priority s. 258 s. 258(3) s. 258(4)

payment or that affects the right of preferential creditors to be paid
s. 258(7) *pari passu* with each other unless those creditors concur. The term 'preferential debt' is given the same meaning as in the context of a liquidation and the 'relevant date' for determining such debts where the debtor is not an undischarged bankrupt is the date of the interim order (see 13.10.2).

s. 259(1) The chairman must prepare a report on the result of the meeting
r. 5.22 and, within four days of the meeting, file a copy of this with the court. At the same time he must give notice of the result to all those who were sent notice of the meeting. The report must state whether or not the proposal was accepted and any modifications that were made; what resolutions were taken and the decisions made on each; which creditors (with their respective values) were at the meeting, whether in person or by proxy, and how they voted on each resolution; and any further information that the chairman thinks appropriate. If
r. 5.24 the meeting approves the proposal, details of the arrangement must
r. 5.23 be lodged with Secretary of State for inclusion in a register available for public inspection.

s. 259(2) If it is reported that the meeting has declined to approve the proposal (whether with or without modifications) the court may discharge any interim order which is in force in relation to the debtor.

9.7 Approval of the proposal

s. 260(2) Where the meeting approves a proposed voluntary arrangement, whether with or without modifications, the approved arrangement will take effect as if made by the debtor at the meeting. Every person who had notice of and was entitled to vote at the meeting, whether or not he actually did so, is bound as if he were a party to the
s. 260(3) composition or scheme. The approved composition or scheme will not be subject to the Deeds of Arrangement Act 1914.

If the debtor is an undischarged bankrupt, the court may take
s. 261(1) either or both of the following courses of action:

(a) The court may annul the bankruptcy order by which the debtor was adjudged bankrupt. Such action may not be taken by the court, however, either before the end of the 28-day period beginning with the day on which the report on the creditors' meeting was made to the court, or at any time when an application to challenge the meeting's decision or an appeal in respect of such an application is pending, or at any time in the period within which such an appeal may be brought.

(b) The court may give such directions as to the conduct of the bankruptcy and the administration of the bankrupt's estate as the court thinks appropriate to facilitate the implementation of the approved composition or scheme.

When a proposal is approved and is not challenged within the 28-day period allowed, any interim order in force in relation to the debtor ceases to have effect. If the court extends the period for challenging the decision, the interim order will cease to have effect at the end of this period. If bankruptcy proceedings have been stayed by an interim order which ceases to have effect in this way, the petition shall be deemed to have been dismissed unless the court orders otherwise. s. 260(4) s. 260(5)

9.8 Challenge of decisions

Within the 28 days beginning with the day on which the report of the creditors' meeting was made to the court, an application challenging the decision may be made either: s. 262(3)

(a) by the debtor; s. 262(2)
(b) by a person entitled to vote at the meeting;
(c) by the nominee or any person who has replaced him; or
(d) if the debtor is an undischarged bankrupt, the trustee of his estate or the official receiver.

The challenge may be made on the ground that the composition or scheme approved at the meeting unfairly prejudices the interest of a creditor and/or that there has been some material irregularity at, or in relation to, the meeting. Apart from this provision, approval given at a meeting will not be invalidated by any irregularity at or in relation to the meeting. s. 262(1)

If the court is satisfied that there is valid ground for the challenge, it may revoke or suspend the approval given by the meeting; or give directions for the summoning of a further meeting of creditors to consider any revised proposal; or, if there was some material irregularity at or in relation to the meeting, direct that the meeting be reconvened to reconsider the original proposal. If, following a direction to summon a further meeting, the court is satisfied that the debtor does not intend to submit a revised proposal it will revoke the direction and revoke or suspend any approval given at the previous meeting. When the court directs that a further meeting be summoned it may continue or renew the period during which the interim order operates and give such supplemental directions as it thinks fit. It may also give supplemental directions when it revokes or suspends an approval. In particular, these directions may relate to things done s. 262(4) s. 262(7) s. 262(6) s. 262(7) since the meeting under any approved composition or scheme and things done which would have been impossible had an interim order been in force.

r. 5.25 The person who challenged the scheme must serve sealed copies of the order made by the court on the supervisor of the arrangement, the debtor and, if applicable, any trustee and the official receiver.

The debtor (or the trustee or official receiver) must then notify creditors and, within seven days, inform the court whether it is intended that a new proposal should be made or that the original scheme should be reconsidered.

9.9 The supervisor

s. 263(2) If a proposal is approved and is not subject to a challenge, the person who is carrying out the functions of the nominee becomes known as
r. 5.20(2) the supervisor of the composition or scheme. If at the meeting it is resolved that a person other than the nominee be supervisor of the arrangement, that person must give the chairman, in writing, his consent to act and confirmation that he is qualified to act as an insolvency practitioner in relation to the debtor. The supervisor
r. 5.21(2) must be put in possession of the assets included in the arrangement and, if the debtor is an undischarged bankrupt, he must
r. 5.21(2) discharge any balance due to the trustee or the official receiver by way of remuneration or on account of any properly incurred fees, costs, charges and expenses and any advances made in respect of the
r. 5.21(3) estate plus interest. As an alternative to immediate payment, the supervisor may give the trustee or the official receiver a written undertaking to discharge any balance outstanding out of the first
r. 5.21(4) realisation of assets. Until he receives payment, the trustee or the official receiver has a charge on the assets covered by the
r. 5.21(5) arrangement, and all guarantees they have properly given for the benefit of the estate must be discharged out of the assets.

s. 263(4) The supervisor acts under the supervision of the court and may apply to the court for directions in relation to any particular matter
s. 263(3) arising under the composition or scheme. Should the debtor or any creditors or any other person be dissatisfied by any act, omission or decision of the supervisor he may apply to the court, which has the power to confirm, reverse or modify any such act or decision. It may also give the supervisor directions or make such other order as it thinks fit.

s. 263(5) In cases where it is both expedient to appoint a person to carry out the functions of the supervisor and inexpedient, difficult or impracticable for such an appointment to be made without the court's assistance, the court may make an order to fill a vacancy, or to increase the number of supervisors, replace a sole supervisor or replace one or more supervisors where there is more than one acting.

The court also retains the power to appoint trustees under s. 41(2) of the Trustee Act 1925.

During the course of the voluntary arrangement the supervisor is required to keep accounts and records of his transactions and, in particular, records of all receipts and payments of money. At a maximum of 12-monthly intervals, the supervisor must prepare an abstract of receipts and payments and, within two months, send a copy to the court, the debtor, and those creditors bound by the arrangement. Together with the abstract, he must also send comments on the progress and efficacy of the arrangement. The Secretary of State may, at any time during the course of the arrangement or after its completion, require the supervisor to produce for inspection his records and accounts, and copies of the abstracts and reports he has prepared. The Secretary of State may order that the accounts and records be audited, and that the supervisor gives such further information and assistance as is necessary for this purpose.

r. 5.26(1)

r. 5.26(2)

r. 5.27

After the arrangement has been completed, the supervisor must, within 28 days, send to all creditors who were bound by the arrangement and to the court, the debtor and the Secretary of State, notice that the arrangement has been fully implemented in accordance with the proposals. This notice must be accompanied by a report summarising all receipts and payments made by the supervisor and giving an explanation of any difference in the actual implementation of the proposal as compared with the proposal as approved by the creditors' meeting.

r. 5.29

Chapter 10

Bankruptcy Proceedings

10.1 Introduction

The Cork Committee (Cmnd 8558) and the White Paper, *A Revised Framework for Insolvency Law* (Cmnd 9175), were at one in thinking that proceedings under the Bankruptcy Act 1914 were too cumbersome. A variety of acts of bankruptcy, most of which were not used in practice, followed by a petition for a receiving order, the involvement of the official receiver, the statement of affairs, public examinations and first meetings of creditors, were all envisaged by the 1914 legislation before adjudication of the bankrupt occurred. In consequence, the Bankruptcy Rules usefully allowed for some short cuts in the process. Only in a minority of cases was a public examination held and in many cases the receiving order and the adjudication order were not separated by the holding of the first meeting of creditors and the public examination.

A new and simplified procedure has been devised. In the case of a creditor's petition, the creditor serves a demand (called a 'statutory demand') upon the debtor which requires the debtor to pay, compound for or secure the debt. If the debtor does not comply within three weeks the creditor may petition the court for a bankruptcy order alleging that the debtor cannot pay his debts because enforcement proceedings have not been fully satisfied; alternatively the petitioner may allege that the debtor has no reasonable prospects of paying his debts because he has not complied with a statutory demand requiring him to show such prospects.

Beneath this beguilingly simple process there hides a problem of some difficulty for debtors, creditors and their advisers. If a creditor 'unreasonably' refuses a composition or security proffered by the debtor in response to the statutory demand the court may in some circumstances refuse the petition. What are creditors and debtors to do? If an insolvent debtor offers the creditor a composition greater than the value of his assets divided into his debts, would the creditor be 'unreasonable' to refuse it? If he is, the petition will be dismissed and the debtor goes on his way still insolvent and at large. If the creditor accepts it, the creditor appears to have been preferred. Threatening creditors, therefore, have every incentive to be first to serve their statutory demands, in order to pressure debtors to offer them an inflated composition greater than other creditors might receive as a means of defending the petition.

If the court makes a bankruptcy order the official receiver takes custody and control of the bankrupt's property. A statement of affairs should be prepared. A public examination will not take place unless either the official receiver or more than half in value of the creditors request it. In the majority of cases the official receiver will have 12 weeks from the date of the bankruptcy order to call a creditors' meeting to choose a trustee in bankruptcy. What was known as a committee of inspection is now called the creditors' committee.

The Act, following the 1914 legislation, contains powers to appoint interim receivers and special managers.

Not every debtor will have to go through the processes outlined above, as there are four main routes along which a debtor may travel:

(a) administration of the debtor's estates by a qualified insolvency practitioner under a voluntary arrangement (see chapter 9);

(b) a scheme of arrangement under the Deeds of Arrangement Act 1914 (which is outside the scope of this work);

(c) a summary administration in bankruptcy (see paragraphs 10.2.4 and 10.6);

(d) the bankruptcy process outlined above.

This chapter deals primarily with the main bankruptcy process under (c) above. The proceedings are dealt with under the following headings:

10.2 The petition
10.3 Consequences of the presentation of a petition
10.4 The bankruptcy order
10.5 Proceedings following a bankruptcy order
10.6 Summary administration.

10.2 The petition

Bankruptcy proceedings commence with a petition for a bankruptcy order presented by any of the following: s. 264

(a) a creditor, or creditors jointly;

(b) the supervisor of a voluntary arrangement made under the Act, or any person (other than the debtor) bound by such an arrangement;

(c) the Director of Public Prosecutions acting as the official petitioner under the Powers of Criminal Courts Act 1973, s. 39(3)(b), where he considers it to be in the public interest to petition;

(d) the debtor himself.

s. 266(2) Once a petition has been presented, it cannot be withdrawn without the leave of the court.

10.2.1 Creditor's petition

The old concept of the acts of bankruptcy has been abolished and
s. 267(2) replaced by the requirement that the debtor appears either to be unable to pay or to have no reasonable prospect of paying the debts specified in the petition.

The apparent inability to pay debts can be shown only by proving either that a statutory demand served upon the debtor to pay, secure or compound for the debt to the petitioner's satisfaction has not been complied with within three weeks (or set aside), or that enforcement
s. 268(1) proceedings upon a judgment debt due to the petitioner have been returned wholly or partly unsatisfied. Where a debt is not immediately payable, the debtor has no reasonable prospect of being able to pay his debts if a statutory demand requiring him to establish reasonable prospects has not been complied with (or set aside).
s. 270 In both cases, the serious possibility of a significant decrease in the debtor's property or its value justifies the presentation of a petition in less than three weeks from the date of the statutory demand.

The following conditions must be satisfied:

s. 265 (a) The debtor must be domiciled or personally present in England and Wales when the petition is presented. A petition may also be presented in respect of a debtor who, during the three years prior to presentation of the petition, was ordinarily resident or had a place of residence in England and Wales or carried on business there, whether personally or by means of an agent or manager, or was a member of a firm or partnership which carried on business in England and Wales.

s. 267(2) and (4) (b) The debt or debts must amount to at least £750 (the 'bankruptcy level') and must be for a liquidated sum payable immediately or at some certain future time.

s. 269(1) (c) The debt must be unsecured. A secured creditor can petition provided that he states in his petition that he is willing to relinquish his security or he can value the security and petition on the unsecured balance.

(d) There is no application pending to set aside a statutory demand on which the petition is based. The court can delete a petitioner's name and continue proceedings with the remaining petitioners and can substitute as petitioner any creditor who has given notice of his intention to appear at the hearing. However, no petition can be withdrawn without the court's leave. Proceedings on a petition can be stayed by the court on such terms as it thinks fit. s. 267(2) s. 271(5) r. 6.30 s. 266(2) r. 6.28 and 6.32

A petition may be dismissed if:

(a) it is appropriate to do so having regard to a breach of the rules or for any other reason;
(b) the debtor is able to pay all his debts (contingent and prospective liabilities are to be taken into account); or
(c) the petitioner has unreasonably refused to accept the debtor's offer (pursuant to a statutory demand) to secure or compound for the debt, which offer would, if accepted, have required the petition to be dismissed.

The court must dismiss a petition if:

(a) the statutory demand to pay, secure or compound has been complied with by the debtor; s. 271(1)
(b) the statutory demand to show a 'reasonable prospect' of being able to pay a debt when due has been complied with by the debtor;
(c) presumably, a petition should not have been 'presented' under the Act because the terms of s. 265 (debtor's domicile, presence etc. in England and Wales) are not satisfied.

10.2.2 Petition by supervisor of a voluntary arrangement (or person bound)

The petition must be based on one of the following grounds: s. 276(1)

(a) that the debtor has failed to comply with his obligations under the arrangement or that he failed to do all such things as the supervisor reasonably required of him; or
(b) that the debtor supplied false or misleading information in a material particular (or which contained material omissions) either in his statement of affairs or other document, or at a creditors' meeting.

10.2.3 Petition by the Director of Public Prosecutions

The Director of Public Prosecutions may, in his capacity as official petitioner, apply under the Powers of Criminal Courts Act 1973 to have declared bankrupt a person convicted of an offence where loss
s. 277(1) above a certain value has been occasioned. His decision must be based on the requirements of the public interest.

The court must make the bankruptcy order on the petition of the official petitioner on production of the criminal bankruptcy order unless it appears that the criminal bankruptcy order has been rescinded on appeal. The court's powers under the Act are not affected by the fact that an appeal against conviction is pending.

10.2.4 Debtor's petition

s. 272(1) and (2) r. 6.68 The only ground for a petition by the debtor himself is that he is unable to pay his debts and the petition must be accompanied by a statement of affairs giving particulars of the debtor's secured and unsecured creditors, his assets and other background information.

s. 265 The debtor must be sufficiently connected with England and Wales for the court to have jurisdiction; see 10.2.1.

Whilst generally the court will make the bankruptcy order sought it must not do so if all the following conditions are satisfied:

s. 273(1) (a) unsecured debts are below an amount for small bankruptcies (£20,000);

(b) the value of the assets is at least of a 'minimum amount' (£2,000);

(c) during the five years before the presentation of the petition the debtor has not been adjudged bankrupt or made a scheme or composition with his creditors; and

(d) it would be appropriate to obtain a report.

s. 273(2) s. 274(2) In these circumstances the court will appoint a qualified insolvency practitioner to inquire into the debtor's affairs and report on the debtor's willingness to propose a voluntary arrangement and whether the creditors should be summoned to consider such proposals (together with a suggested time and place for the creditors' meeting). On considering the report the court may make an interim order under s. 252 to enable the proposals to be considered and implemented. Unless the court directs otherwise, a meeting of creditors can be summoned as proposed, and the proceedings then follow the rules laid down for a voluntary arrangement (see chapter 9). Alternatively, the court may make a bankruptcy order.

If a bankruptcy order is made and the conditions in (a) and (c) above are met, the court may issue a certificate for the summary administration of the debtor's estate. The consequences of this are outlined in paragraph 10.6.

10.3 Consequences of the presentation of a petition

10.3.1 Restrictions on dispositions of property

Any disposition of property or payment of money made after the — s. 284(1)
petition is presented is void in the event that a bankruptcy order is — and (2)
made, subject to court approval and certain exceptions; this is dealt with later in 12.2.

10.3.2 Restrictions upon proceedings against the debtor

The court can stay any action, execution or legal process against the — s. 285(1)
property or person of any debtor while bankruptcy proceedings are
pending. These powers apply to property which would not form part — s. 285(6)
of the debtor's estate even if he were to be adjudged bankrupt. The
court may act simply on proof of the presentation of a bankruptcy — s. 285(2)
petition.

10.3.3 Interim receivers

Where a petition has been presented, the debtor or a creditor (or an — s. 286(1)
insolvency practitioner appointed under s. 273(2)) may apply to the court for the appointment of an interim receiver for the protection of the debtor's estate. The official receiver will be the interim receiver or, where the petition was presented by the debtor and a qualified
insolvency practitioner has been appointed to report on the debtor's — s. 286(2)
affairs, the court may appoint the reporting practitioner.

An interim receiver has such powers as the court decides to allow — s. 286(3)
him but in the absence of any restrictions imposed by the court he will have all the powers available to the official receiver when acting
as receiver after a bankruptcy order has been made. These powers are — s. 287(2)
all the powers available to a receiver and manager appointed by the High Court, and the power to sell perishable goods, and goods that are likely to diminish in value if not sold. The interim receiver shall
also take all steps necessary to protect the estate but if expenditure is — s. 287(3)
to be incurred the Secretary of State's permission is needed.

In any event the interim receiver must take immediate possession — s. 286(4)
of the property that he has been appointed to receive and he is
entitled to the debtor's assistance. — s. 286(5)

10.3.4 Special manager

After a petition has been presented, application may be made to the — s. 370(2)
court by the official receiver or the trustee for the appointment of a special manager where such appointment is required by the nature of

the debtor's estate, property or business or by the interests of the creditors; the application must be supported by a report setting out
r. 6.167 the reasons. The court order will specify the duration of the appointment, which may be renewed. Other matters affecting a special manager are:

s. 370(3) (a) His powers will be defined by the court.
r. 6.167(4) (b) Remuneration will be fixed by the court.
r. 6.168 (c) The appointment does not take effect until security has been given.
r. 6.170 (d) He must keep receipts and payments, and produce them at least every three months to the trustee.
r. 6.171 (e) There are specified circumstances in which the appointment may be terminated.

10.4 The bankruptcy order

10.4.1 Power of the court to make a bankruptcy order

The court's power to make a bankruptcy order is discretionary. The fact that the petition is lodged in the wrong court is not fatal, and
s. 373 proceedings commenced in the wrong court may be transferred to the appropriate court.

s. 375 If the debtor wishes to appeal from an order made in a county court he should apply to a single judge of the High Court and from there, with leave, he may appeal to the Court of Appeal.

10.4.2 Effect of a bankruptcy order upon the debtor

The debtor is now an undischarged bankrupt and by virtue of s. 283 he is deprived of the ownership of his property (assets in the
s. 291(1)(a) bankruptcy are dealt with in chapter 12). The bankrupt must give up
and (b) possession of his estate, hand over all books, papers and other records in his possession which relate to his estate or affairs
s. 291(2) (including documents to which privilege attaches) and he must do all things which may reasonably be required of him to protect property which is not in his possession or to enable such property to be
s. 291(4) recovered. He must, furthermore, make an inventory of his estate, give other information and attend upon the official receiver to the extent that may reasonably be required, for the breach of which duties he may be made liable as for a contempt of court.

s. 366(1) The official receiver or the trustee in bankruptcy can apply at any
and (2) time to have the bankrupt questioned in court on pain of arrest and liability to seizure of books, papers, records, goods or money if he fails without reasonable excuse to appear or if he absconds (or there is reason to believe he may abscond). Powers of arrest and seizure of

books, papers, records, money or goods also exist if there is reason to believe that the bankrupt is about to destroy, remove or conceal such books, papers etc. (or has already done so) or if he has, without leave, removed property with a value exceeding £500. s. 364(2) SI 1986 No. 1996

Powers to break into property to recover or seize assets, books, papers or records are also available against the bankrupt. It should be noted in passing that the powers under ss. 365 and 366 extend, where appropriate, to other persons who can supply information or who are under a duty to deliver up books, property etc. This includes the bankrupt's spouse or former spouse. s. 365 s. 366(1)

Purported dispositions of his property by the bankrupt are avoided subject only to the exceptions listed in s. 284(5)(a) and (b) (protection for bankers and others) and s. 284(6) (dispositions of property held by the bankrupt on trust).

The bankrupt may also have his mail redirected by order of the court. Whilst undischarged the bankrupt cannot sit and vote in the House of Lords or House of Commons and he is not eligible for election to the latter. s. 371 s. 427

10.5 Proceedings following a bankruptcy order

10.5.1 Official receiver becomes receiver and manager of the estate

Immediately upon the making of a bankruptcy order the official receiver becomes receiver and manager of the bankrupt's estate pending the appointment of a trustee in bankruptcy. This rule, however, is subject to a number of exceptions. These exceptional cases arise when a trustee in bankruptcy is appointed at the time when the bankruptcy order is made and are as follows: s. 287

(a) In the case of criminal bankruptcy proceedings the official receiver becomes trustee immediately upon the making of the bankruptcy order. s. 297(1)

(b) In a small bankruptcy (i.e., a summary administration) the official receiver becomes trustee immediately. s. 292(1)

(c) Where a debtor has petitioned against himself the court appoints a qualified insolvency practitioner to report on the debtor's position and if the court adjudges the debtor bankrupt it may there and then appoint the insolvency practitioner as trustee. s. 297(4)

(d) Where the basis of the bankruptcy order is non-compliance with the terms of a scheme or composition, the supervisor of the scheme or composition may be appointed as trustee at the time when the bankruptcy order is made. s. 297(5)

The official receiver has all the powers of a receiver or manager appointed by the High Court and he can sell perishable goods or s. 287(2) goods which will diminish in value if not sold. He may also take all steps which he thinks fit for the protection of the debtor's property.

s. 287(3) He must not, however, incur expenditure without obtaining permission from the Secretary of State.

s. 287(4) The Act gives the official receiver protection should he accidentally seize or dispose of an asset which does not belong to the debtor. If the official receiver had reasonable grounds to believe that the asset did form part of the debtor's property and if he was not negligent, no liability will be incurred by him in respect of the disposition or seizure, and he has a lien on the property or the proceeds of its sale for expenses incurred.

Whilst acting as receiver and manager under s. 287 the official s. 289(1) and (4) receiver must also investigate the conduct and affairs of the bankrupt including matters which occurred before the date of the bankruptcy order.

s. 289(1) The official receiver need only report on his investigation if he thinks fit. If he does report, the report he makes is prima facie evidence of the matters contained in it.

10.5.2 Statement of affairs

The bankrupt must prepare a statement of affairs, and submit s. 288(1) it to the official receiver within 21 days of the bankruptcy order. The requirement does not apply when the debtor petitions against himself, since he will have prepared a statement earlier for submission with his petition.

s. 288(3) The official receiver can dispense with the need for a statement of affairs altogether but if he declines to exercise his discretion to extend time or dispense with the statement he can be overridden by the court.

r. 6.59 The statement must set out details of the bankrupt's secured and unsecured creditors, and his assets.

10.5.3 Public examination

s. 290(1) At any time after the making of a bankruptcy order and before the bankrupt's discharge the official receiver can apply to the court for the public examination of the bankrupt.

s. 290(2) If the official receiver makes no application of his own motion, the creditors, provided at least half of them in value agree, can require him to apply for such an examination.

s. 290(3), (4) and (5) Where an examination is ordered, the bankrupt must attend (he commits a contempt of court if he fails to do so without reasonable excuse) and answer questions on his affairs, dealings and property and the cause of his failure.

Those who take part in the public examination are the official receiver, the official petitioner (in criminal bankruptcy cases only), the trustee in bankruptcy of the bankrupt, the special manager and any creditor who has proved his debt.

10.5.4 Appointment of a special manager

The official receiver (or the trustee in bankruptcy) may apply to the court for the appointment of a special manager under s. 370; the rules relating to special managers are summarised in 10.3.4.

10.5.5 Title of a trustee in bankruptcy

The official title is 'trustee of the estate of . . ., a bankrupt' but s. 305(4)
reference may be made to the appointee as 'trustee in bankruptcy' of the bankrupt.

10.5.6 Appointment of a creditors' committee

The creditors may appoint a creditors' committee, unless the trustee s. 301
in bankruptcy is the official receiver, in which latter case the functions exercisable by the committee shall be exercised by the Secretary of State.

10.6 Summary administration

As noted in 10.2.4, if certain conditions are met, the court may issue a s. 275
certificate of summary administration. The effect of this is that the official receiver immediately takes on the office of trustee, and s. 297(2)
proceeds with the administration of the estate. However, at any time a certificate is in force, the court may appoint a person other than the s. 297(3)
official receiver to act as trustee.

The official receiver must, within 12 months after the issue of the r. 6.49
certificate, inform creditors of the making of the bankruptcy order, and the obligation to decide whether or not to call a meeting of creditors (dealt with generally in 11.2) remains.

Where a certificate of summary administration is in force, the official receiver's duty to investigate the bankrupt's affairs is s. 289(5)
discretionary.

A certificate of summary administration may be revoked by the s. 275(3)
court at any time if it appears that the certificate ought not to have been issued.

Chapter 11

The Trustee in Bankruptcy

11.1 Introduction

The Act follows the previous law in providing for the administration of the bankrupt's estate by a trustee in bankruptcy, but the trustee must now be a qualified insolvency practitioner unless he is the official receiver.

The functions, powers and duties attached to the office are broadly similar to those contained in the Bankruptcy Act 1914, although the trustee may now employ a solicitor without obtaining the sanction of the creditors' committee.

The right to make the trustee account for, or restore, property and make good losses caused by breaches of fiduciary or other duty seems to have been freed from some of the restraints imposed by judicial interpretation of the Bankruptcy Act 1914.

The law is set out under the following headings:

11.2 Appointment by creditors
11.3 Appointment by others
11.4 Functions, duties and powers
11.5 Control over the trustee
11.6 Resignation and removal
11.7 Release of the trustee

11.2 Appointment by creditors

s. 293 Where the official receiver acts as receiver and manager after the making of the bankruptcy order he has 12 weeks in which to decide whether or not to call a creditors' meeting to have a trustee in bankruptcy appointed. If he decides to call it, then during that period
r. 6.79(1) of 12 weeks he must fix a venue for the meeting to be held within
s. 293(2) four months of the bankruptcy order. He must hold a meeting, if a quarter in value of the creditors properly request it, within three
r. 6.79(2) months of the creditors' request. Once the date of the meeting has

been fixed the official receiver must forthwith notify the court. Notice must be given to every creditor shown in the statement of affairs or known to the official receiver at least 21 days before the date of the meeting, and the notice must be accompanied by a proof
of debt and a proxy form. The meeting has to be held between 10 a.m. r. 6.86(3)
and 4 p.m. on a business day (unless the court directs otherwise), at a r. 6.86(2)
place having regard to the convenience of creditors. The notice of the r. 6.86(1)
meeting must also be advertised.

The purpose of the first creditors' meeting is to appoint a trustee r. 6.80
and to establish a creditors' committee but, if no such committee is established, the meeting may also consider the basis of the trustee's
remuneration. The meeting will be chaired by the official receiver, or r. 6.82(1)
someone nominated by him. The chairman has the power to admit or r. 6.94
reject all or part of a creditors' proof for the purpose of his entitlement to vote. If the chairman is unsure whether to admit or reject a proof he must mark it as objected and allow the creditor to vote, subject to the vote being declared invalid if the objection is later upheld.

The quorum for a meeting is three creditors present in person or by r. 6.92
proxy (or all creditors if there are only three or less) although either the chairman or any creditor may alone constitute a quorum by virtue of proxies held.

A creditor is entitled to vote only if he has lodged, by the time and r. 6.93
date specified in the notice, a proof of debt, which has been admitted by the chairman, and, if applicable, a form of proxy. There is no voting right for unliquidated debts or for those whose value is unascertained unless the chairman estimates a minimum value for them. A secured creditor must deduct the estimated value of his security from his claim, and can vote only in respect of the balance, if any.

At the meeting, a resolution is passed if a majority in value (of r. 6.88
those voting) vote in favour; proxy votes are included. On a resolution to appoint a trustee, if there are two nominees the person who obtains the most support is appointed. However, where there are three or more nominations, the person to be appointed has to achieve a clear majority over the others taken together, and if this is not achieved on the first vote, further votes must be taken with the person who achieved the least support dropping out at each stage.

The appointed trustee must confirm in writing his qualification r. 6.120
and consent to act to the chairman of the creditors' meeting, who then certifies the appointment. The certificate is filed by the official
receiver in court (date to be endorsed upon it) and returned to him s. 292(4)
for delivery to the trustee. The date given in the endorsement by the and
court is the date of appointment. r. 6.120

r. 6.91 The meeting may be adjourned for up to 21 days; an adjournment must occur if a quorum is not present within 30 minutes of the time set for the meeting.

r. 6.95 The chairman of the meeting must keep minutes, and details of any resolutions passed must be filed in court within 21 days of the meeting. The chairman must also prepare a list of all creditors present at the meeting.

11.3 Appointment by others

11.3.1 The court

The power of appointment is excercisable by the court in the following circumstances:

s. 297(3) (a) In a summary administration the court can appoint someone other than the official receiver when making the bankruptcy order.

s. 297(4) (b) If a bankruptcy order is made following a report to the court by an insolvency practitioner (debtor's own petition) that person may be appointed as trustee.

s. 297(5) (c) If a bankruptcy order is made when a voluntary arrangement is in force, the supervisor may be appointed.

r. 6.121 In these cases a written statement of qualification and consent must be filed in court. Two copies of the order are sent to the official receiver, one of which (sealed by the official receiver) he sends to the trustee, and the appointment is effective from the date of the order.

11.3.2 The Secretary of State

An appointment may be made by the Secretary of State, upon referral by the official receiver:

s. 296 (a) at any time when the official receiver is acting as trustee (other than in cases of criminal bankruptcy);

s. 300 (b) where there is a vacancy in the office of trustee, and no creditors' meeting is to be held;

s. 295 (c) at the discretion of the official receiver, where no appointment is made at the first creditors' meeting.

r. 6.122 and s. 292 The Secretary of State sends two copies of the appointment to the official receiver for transmission to the court and to the appointee, and the appointment is effective from the date specified in the Secretary of State's certificate.

11.3.3 Statutory appointment

In criminal bankruptcy proceedings the official receiver must be the trustee in bankruptcy as from the making of the bankruptcy order. s. 297

11.4 Functions, duties and powers

11.4.1 Functions

The functions of the trustee in bankruptcy are to get in, realise and distribute the bankrupt's estate and he may exercise discretion as to how to perform those functions. s. 305(2)

11.4.2 Duties

The principal duties are:

(a) to take possession of books, papers and other records relating to the bankrupt's affairs; s. 311

(b) to notify the creditors' committee of the employment of a solicitor; s. 314(6)(c)

(c) to notify the creditors' committee of all disposals of property to the bankrupt's associates; s. 314(6)(b)

(d) to distribute dividends;

(e) to convene meetings of creditors if one tenth in value request it; s. 314(7)

(f) to pay costs, fees and expenses in the order prescribed (see 13.7); r. 6.224

(g) upon receiving notice of the presentation of a second bankruptcy petition, to refrain from disposing of assets or income or paying dividends; s. 334

(h) to keep, produce and submit for audit his books, records and accounts; IReg, regs 8-13

(i) to pay money into the Insolvency Services Account kept by the Secretary of State with the Bank of England unless authorised not to;

(j) to summon final meetings of creditors when the administration for practical purposes is complete. s. 331

11.4.3 Powers

The trustee can:

(a) exercise all the powers of a High Court receiver to get in or retain the estate; s. 311(2)

(b) apply for appointment of a special manager; s. 370

(c) transfer shares, stock or other property transferable in the s. 311(3) books of any company, office or person to the same extent as the bankrupt could;

s. 311(5) (d) serve notice to inspect goods pawned, pledged or similarly secured to see whether or not to redeem;

s. 312 (e) require delivery up or production for inspection of books, papers, documents or records;

s. 371 (f) have the bankrupt's mail redirected;

s. 349 (g) override liens on books, papers or records enjoyed by third parties unless held as a document of title;

s. 369 (h) obtain a court order directing the Inland Revenue to produce returns, accounts and assessments or correspondence;

(i) inspect Land Registry entries;

s. 372 (j) demand supplies of electricity, gas, water and telecommunication services without paying arrears;

s. 290 (k) take part in the bankrupt's public examination;

s. 363 (l) apply to the court for orders directing the bankrupt to do any act in relation to the administration of the estate;

s. 348 (m) return premiums in respect of unexpired periods of training of apprentices and articled clerks;

s. 310 (n) apply for an income payments order;

s. 314

sch. 5, pt II (o) sell any part of the estate;

ibid. (p) give effective receipts;

ibid. (q) prove, rank, claim and draw dividends in estates of debtors of his bankrupt;

ibid. (r) exercise all powers over property vested in him;

ibid. (s) deal with entails as the bankrupt might have done;

sch. 5, pt III (t) hold property, make contracts, sue, be sued, bind himself by engagements, employ agents, execute documents, deeds, powers of attorney and do any other necessary or expedient thing for the above powers;

s. 314(7) (u) call creditors' meetings.

With the sanction of the creditors' committee the trustee may:

sch. 5, pt I (a) carry on the business for beneficial winding up;

ibid. (b) bring or defend legal proceedings in respect of the bankrupt's property;

ibid. (c) accept promises of future payment on a sale of the bankrupt's property subject to such security as the creditors' committee demands;

ibid. (d) mortgage or pledge assets to raise money;

ibid. (e) make payments or incur liabilities in order to secure any rights, options or powers for the benefit of creditors that the bankrupt had;

(f) take arbitration, or compromise debts due to the estate; ibid.

(g) appoint the bankrupt to do particular acts in the management or carrying on of the bankrupt's business (approval must be given in advance for this, except in emergencies); s. 314(2) and (3)

(h) divide property *in specie* if it cannot readily or advantageously be sold. s. 326

11.4.4 Disclaimer of onerous property

The trustee in bankruptcy also has the power to disclaim onerous property, that is, unprofitable contracts, property that is unsaleable or not readily saleable, and property that may give rise to a liability to pay money or perform onerous acts. s. 315

The effect of the disclaimer is to determine all rights, liabilities and interests of the bankrupt in the property and to discharge (retrospectively) the trustee from any personal liability. However, the disclaimer does not affect the rights and liabilities of any other person in such property. After-acquired property claimed by notice under ss. 307 to 309 cannot be disclaimed subsequently without the leave of the court. Equally where the trustee has claimed tools of the trade, household equipment etc., on the ground that its value exceeded the cost of a reasonable replacement, the court's permission is needed to disclaim. s. 315(3) s. 315(4)

Where leases are disclaimed a copy of the disclaimer must be served upon every person claiming under the bankrupt as a mortgagee or underlessee and such persons have 14 days in which to apply to the court for orders as to the vesting of the property and the terms and conditions of its vesting (so that any person in whom the disclaimed property is vested is subject to the same rights and liabilities as the bankrupt or the same obligations which would arise if the property had been assigned to him on that day). s. 317 s. 321(1)

The court may make such order as it thinks fit with regard to tenant's improvements and fixtures where it orders the disclaimer. s. 317

If no person is willing to accept an order of the court because of the terms or conditions which would be imposed by s. 321(1) the court may vest it in any person liable to perform the lessee's covenants in the lease but free from all estates, incumbrances and interests created by the bankrupt. Pressure may be brought to bear, however, on persons who find s. 321(1) not to their liking in that anyone refusing a vesting order is excluded from all interest in the property. s. 321(4)

Any person who suffers loss or damage through a disclaimer may prove against the bankrupt's estate for the value of the loss. Where s. 315(5)

land subject to a rentcharge vests in the Crown or other persons by
s. 319 virtue of the disclaimer and the operation of any rule of law, no liability attaches to the Crown or other persons until it or they take possession or control or enter into occupation of the property.

s. 316 The trustee in bankruptcy must make an election to disclaim or not, if he is served with a written notice by any person interested in property requiring him to decide, and if the trustee makes no election within 28 days of the notice he is deemed to have adopted the contract or property, thereby losing all further right to disclaim.

11.5 Control over the trustee

A trustee in bankruptcy is subject to control by other persons or bodies. Indeed every bankruptcy is subject to the control of the court which can settle all priorities and all questions of fact and law. A restraining hand is kept over a trustee in several ways:

r. 6.148 (a) He must not solicit office improperly and may forfeit his remuneration if he does so.

r. 6.138-142 (b) He must comply with rules dealing with his remuneration, which must not be excessive.

r. 6.146 (c) On ceasing to act through resignation, removal, or cesser of qualification he must forthwith hand over all assets, books, papers, correspondence etc. to the succeeding trustee.

r. 6.149 (d) He must give all information and assistance to the official receiver and permit inspection of books and records.

s. 303 (e) Anyone who is dissatisfied with any act or decision of the trustee can apply to the court.

r. 6.147 (f) He must not enter into transactions with an associate of his without prior consent from the court and must behave equitably.

s. 304 (g) He can be made liable for misapplying or retaining assets or in respect of breach of duty or breach of trust.

(h) The creditors' threat to remove him from office may keep a restraint upon him.

11.6 Resignation and removal

11.6.1 Resignation

Resignation is possible on grounds of ill-health; intended cessation
r. 6.126(3) of practice; conflict of interest; or a change of personal circumstances precluding or making impracticable a continuation in office. A creditors' meeting must be convened, notice of which summarises the
r. 6.126(1) and (2) trustee's receipts and payments and declares that his account with the Secretary of State reconciles. The notice must state the object of

the meeting and refer to the rules as to release (r. 6.135). If the resignation is accepted, the chairman sends a copy of the resolution and a certificate to the official receiver within three days. The resigning trustee must also notify the official receiver forthwith, and file the notice in court and send a copy to the official receiver within three days (accompanied by copies of the account). The official receiver files a copy in court which becomes the effective time of resignation.

If the creditors do not accept the resignation, the trustee may apply to the court, and the court can deal with the matter as it thinks fit. r. 6.128

11.6.2 Removal

In general, a trustee can be removed from office either by the court or by a general meeting of creditors summoned for the purpose. However, the ability to summon a creditors' meeting is restricted where: s. 298(1) s. 298(4)

(a) the official receiver acts as trustee because of the failure by creditors to make an appointment; or
(b) the appointment was made by the court (other than in connection with a voluntary arrangement); or
(c) the appointment was made by the Secretary of State.

In such cases the meeting can be held only if the trustee agrees, the court directs, or on requisition by not less than one quarter in value of creditors. Further, such a meeting cannot be held in a summary administration. s. 298(3)

If a meeting of creditors is held, any resolution must be notified to the official receiver, and removal is effective from the date endorsed on the official receiver's certificate of removal. In any event, in a criminal bankruptcy the official receiver cannot be removed from office. r. 6.131 s. 298(2)

The Secretary of State may remove any trustee appointed by him. s. 298(5) r. 6.133

11.6.3 Annulment of bankruptcy order

The trustee vacates office where the bankruptcy order is annulled. s. 298(9)

11.6.4 Loss of qualification to be an insolvency practitioner

The trustee vacates office upon becoming unqualified to act in the bankruptcy. s. 298(6)

11.6.5 Notice after final creditors' meeting

The trustee vacates office after he files in court a notice that the final s. 298(8) meeting of creditors following completion of the administration has been held.

11.7 Release of the trustee

s. 299(5) Release involves the trustee in discharge from all personal liability in respect of his acts or omissions in the administration of the estate and his conduct as trustee. Any liability for misfeasance, breach of trust or breach of duty, however, may be imposed under s.304 despite release.

The official receiver is released at the time when, having been
s. 299(1)(a) and (b) replaced by a nominee of the Secretary of State or the creditors, he gives notice of that fact to the court. If his release follows upon completion of the administration the Secretary of State settles the
r. 6.136 time of release (notice of intent to apply for release and a summary of receipts and payments as trustee must first be sent to all proving creditors and the bankrupt).

Trustees other than the official receiver who resign or who are removed by the creditors without a resolution against their release
r. 6.127 are released when their resignations or removals are effective. In
r. 6.137 cases where the administration is complete and there is no resolution against release at the final meeting of creditors, the release operates from the time when the trustee notifies the court of the creditors' meeting decision and his report thereon.

s. 299 If the creditors have resolved against release, the trustee must apply to the Secretary of State, who will settle the matter. In other
r. 6.135 cases the Secretary of State settles the time of release. Where the bankruptcy is annulled the court settles release after final accounts
s. 299 are filed with the Secretary of State and the court.

Chapter 12

Assets in the Bankruptcy

12.1 Introduction

The Act is primarily designed, as were its predecessors, to give the creditors the benefit of the assets of the bankrupt in the estate at the time of his adjudication, and his after-acquired property.

The law is set out under the following headings:

12.2 Avoidance of dispositions after presentation of a petition

Any disposition of property or payment of money by the bankrupt after the presentation of the petition and up to the vesting of the s. 284(3) estate in the trustee in bankruptcy (i.e., the time of appointment stated in the certificate of appointment) is void unless approved by s. 284(1) the court before or after the disposition or payment.

In the absence of the court's approval the person to whom the money or property was transferred holds it as part of the debtor's estate. Furthermore this rule applies even though the property or s. 284(6) money transferred would not have formed part of the debtor's estate at all. One useful saving is provided in s. 284(6) which allows dispositions of any trust property held by the debtor to stand.

This general rule might cause hardship in circumstances where a person deals with the debtor without being aware that a petition has been presented against the debtor. The Act gives limited protection s. 284(4) to persons dealing with the debtor during the period between the presentation of the petition and the making of the bankruptcy order by denying any recourse against such persons where they acted in

good faith, for value and without notice of the presentation of the petition. Any person who subsequently acquires that property from a protected person or acquires an interest in such property is likewise shielded from s. 284(1) and (2). It should be noted that the limited protection described above does not apply to dispositions and payments made after the commencement of bankruptcy (i.e., after
s. 278 the date of the bankruptcy order) except where the bankrupt has
s. 284(5) incurred a debt to a banker or other person by making a payment
s. 284 avoided by s. 284 and either the banker or other person had no notice of the bankruptcy and the person to whom the money was paid was someone from whom it was not reasonably practicable to recover the payment. This exception is an adaptation of the old s. 4 of the Bankruptcy (Amendment) Act 1926 which was designed to avoid some of the effects of *Re Wigzell* [1921] 2 KB 835.

The Act refers to 'dispositions' and 'payments' and *not* to contracts for dispositions and payments. Any incomplete transactions cannot be enforced, and the other party's only remedies will be a possible proof for damages for non-performance or an application for discharge from the contract on such terms as the court thinks equitable under s. 345.

12.3 Nature of the trustee's title

12.3.1 Commencement of title

The date of succession to the bankrupt's estate is 'the commence-
s. 278(a) ment of bankruptcy' (i.e., the date of the bankruptcy order), but the
s. 306(1) property vests in the trustee only when his appointment takes effect. Where the official receiver is trustee the property vests at the time of his becoming trustee.

Thus a form of relation back of the trustee's title is produced by the Act — though nothing like the doctrine of relation back under of the 1914 Act. The period of relation back could amount to almost three
s. 293(1) months as, after adjudication, the official receiver has 12 weeks in
r. 6.120 which to hold a creditors' meeting to appoint a trustee and the latter has to accept his appointment (which he does by providing the chairman of the creditors' meeting with a written statement of his qualification as an insolvency practitioner and consent to act), which the chairman then certifies. The appointment then takes effect from the date that the certificate is filed in court. A trustee appointed
r. 6.121 by the court supplies like statements to the court and the appointment takes effect from the date of the court order.

s. 307 As far as property acquired by the bankrupt after his adjudication
s. 333(2) is concerned, the trustee must claim it from the bankrupt by notice served within 42 days of it first coming to his knowledge. The debtor

must give notice to the trustee within 21 days of becoming aware of r. 6.200
the acquisition. A bankrupt who disposes of such property without s. 309(1)
first notifying the trustee must give all relevant details to enable the r. 6.200(3)
trustee to recover the property. If the trustee does not act within 42 days he must apply to the court (knowledge of any predecessor trustee counts in the calculation of a successor trustee's 42-day
period). The trustee's title then operates from the date of acquisition s. 307(3)
by the bankrupt unless, in the meantime, the property was s. 307(4)
transferred to a bona fide purchaser for value without notice of the bankruptcy.

The bankrupt's estate includes the capacity to exercise, and take
proceedings for exercising, all powers over or in respect of property s. 283(4)
for the benefit of the bankrupt whilst undischarged.

The vesting of the property in the trustee is automatic under the s. 306(2)
Act — documents, conveyances etc. are not necessary. Property abroad may need formalities under foreign law and the trustee can compel the bankrupt to take all steps as may be required to vest the property (refusal without reasonable excuse is a contempt of court).

12.3.2 Scope of the trustee's title

The trustee takes the estate 'subject to the rights of any person other s. 283(5)
than the bankrupt (whether as secured creditor or otherwise) in relation thereto'.

12.4 Property belonging to the bankrupt that is available

The bankrupt's estate comprises 'all property belonging to or vested s. 283(1)
in the bankrupt at the commencement of the bankruptcy'.
Property includes 'money, goods, things in action, land and every s. 436
description of property wherever situated, and also obligations and every description of interest, whether present or future or vested or contingent, arising out of, or incidental to, property'.

12.5 Assets belonging to the bankrupt that are not available

12.5.1 General

The following are excluded from the trustee's estate: tools, books,
vehicles and other items of equipment necessary to the bankrupt for s. 283(2)
use personally by him in his employment or business and such personal and household items as are necessary for satisfying the basic domestic needs of the bankrupt and his family (unless under s. 308 the trustee serves notice to claim any such items whose realisable value exceeds the cost of a reasonable replacement).

Property held by the bankrupt on trust for any other person is s. 283(3) excluded, as is the right of nomination to a vacant ecclesiastical benefice.

12.5.2 Bankrupt's personal earnings

The trustee can ask the court for an income payments order, s. 310 although the court must leave a sufficient amount for the reasonable domestic needs of the bankrupt and his family. These may be ordered to be paid by the bankrupt or the payer of the income. 'Income' here includes every payment in the nature of income and covers any payment in respect of the carrying on of any business, or in respect of any office or employment.

The bankrupt is entitled to 28 days' notice of the court hearing and r. 6.189 he must be informed at least seven days before the hearing that he is required to attend unless he gives written consent to the order sought.

Variation of the order is possible and the bankrupt must notify the r. 6.200(1) trustee of any change in his income within 21 days of becoming aware of the change. Further if the bankrupt carries on a business he must r. 6.200(5) supply six-monthly summaries of purchases and sales, and the profit or loss arising.

12.5.3 Rights of action

The provisions of s. 283, 311(4) and 436 of the Act correspond closely with s. 38(a), 48(5) and 167 of the Bankruptcy Act 1914 under which rights of personal action remained in the ownership of the bankrupt (e.g., damages for injury to credit) and actions for damages for injury to property vested in the trustee and those of a mixed character could be split.

12.5.4 Peerages and titles of honour

These do not pass to the trustee under the Act even though they are regarded as freehold property.

12.5.5 Interests defeasible on bankruptcy

The law operating under the 1914 Act has not been changed and will continue to apply under the Act. The principle is that forfeiture and defeasance clauses will be construed strictly but if they do not amount to a fraud on the creditors the trustee is bound by such clauses and the estate will exclude, because it cannot include, property interests defeasible on bankruptcy. See *Mackintosh* v *Pogose* [1895] 1 Ch 505.

12.6 Property not belonging to the bankrupt that is available

12.6.1 Preferences

A transaction is a preference actionable by the trustee in bankruptcy if a debtor:

(a) does anything or suffers anything to be done that has the effect of putting a creditor, or surety, or guarantor for any of his debts or liabilities into a position which, in the event of his bankruptcy, will be better than if that thing had not been done or suffered; and s. 340

(b) was insolvent at the time; and

(c) was influenced by a desire to produce the effect of putting such creditor, guarantor or surety into that better position.

The period during which transactions are vulnerable varies according to the circumstances:

(a) If the transaction is at an undervalue (see below) five years before the presentation of the petition. s. 341(1)(a)

(b) If the transaction is not at an undervalue and is entered into with an associate of the debtor, two years before the presentation of the petition. An associate is defined by s. 435 as the bankrupt's spouse or former or reputed spouse, and, in relation to any of them or the bankrupt, a brother, sister, uncle, aunt, nephew, niece, lineal ancestor or lineal descendant (including half-blood and stepchildren and adopted children: illegitimate children count as legitimate children). Equally a company controlled by the bankrupt or any associate(s) as defined above is an associate; control includes cases where the board of a company or of any company which controls it, acts customarily in accordance with a person's instructions and includes cases where a person can exercise one third of the voting power of the company or of any other company which controls it. s. 341(1)(b)

(c) Where the person preferred is not an associate and the transaction is not at an undervalue, six months before the presentation of the petition. s. 341(1)(c)

In the case of preferences to associates, influence is presumed until disproved. A person is insolvent if he cannot from his own resources meet his debts and liabilities as they fall due, or if the value of his assets is less than the amount of his liabilities, taking into account contingent and prospective liabilities. The fact that something is done in pursuance of a court order does not prevent that thing from being an actionable preference. Thus, for example, if an insolvent s. 340(5) s. 341(3) s. 340(6) debtor arranges with a creditor to submit to a judgment for the debt in order to give the creditor the benefit of the charge over the debtor's assets conferred by enforcement proceedings, the transaction is nonetheless capable of being an actionable preference.

The phrase 'influenced by a desire' to put the creditor into a better position has no previous history in bankruptcy law. How much influence should the desire exert if it is to be actionable? The desire to improve the creditor's position might be the sole influencing factor or it may be the dominant one when the debtor acts otherwise than single-mindedly, or it might be of minor significance. Decisions of the courts will be necessary to interpret this phrase.

The court's powers to redress preferences are wide and can involve vesting or revesting property, reviving or making fresh obligations, requiring payments and making charges.

Such orders therefore can affect property in the hands of third parties. Two categories of third party, however, are beyond the court's power:

s. 342(2) (a) any person who bona fide for value and without notice of the relevant circumstances acquires property from another who acquired such property as a party to the preference; and

(b) any person receiving a benefit in good faith for value and without notice of the relevant circumstances.

12.6.2 Transactions at an undervalue

s. 341(1)(a) and s. 339 If during five years before presentation of the petition the bankrupt, whilst insolvent, has entered into any transaction at an undervalue, the court can remedy the matter, using the powers and protections available in the case of preferences set out above, on the application of the trustee.

s. 339(3) A transaction is at an undervalue if:

(a) it is a gift by the bankrupt; or

(b) the bankrupt received no consideration; or

(c) the bankrupt entered into the transaction in consideration of marriage; or

(d) the bankrupt received consideration which in money or money's worth was significantly less in value than that provided.

No mental state on the part of the bankrupt need be proved.

s. 342 The court's remedy is to be directed to restoring the parties to their original positions.

12.6.3 Transactions defrauding creditors

The Law of Property Act 1925, s. 172, is repealed and replaced by s. 423.

There are two elements in a defrauding transaction:

(a) A transaction at an undervalue by the bankrupt.

(b) An intention by the relevant person to put assets beyond the reach of actual or potential claimants against the relevant person or an intention otherwise to prejudice the interests of such claimants.

Those who may apply to the court when there is a bankruptcy are the official receiver and the trustee in bankruptcy, but victims of a transaction can apply only with the leave of the court. One interesting development under the Act is that such applications are to be treated as made on behalf of every person who is, or is capable of being, prejudiced by the transaction and are, therefore, representative actions in substance. The representative nature of the action is reinforced in terms of remedy. The court's powers to order a revesting of property and to follow any proceeds of sale or a payment are both expressed to be for the benefit of all persons on whose behalf the application is made. The powers to release or discharge security, to order payments by those who have benefited, to renew or revive suretyships or guarantee obligations and to direct security to be given to discharge obligations under the order and to order such security to replace a security released or discharged by the impugned transaction, are not expressed to be for the benefit of all; but in so far as there is a community of interest amongst some or all of the creditors the court can preserve that community of interest in its order. There are savings for certain bona fide third parties in s. 425 under applications in respect of an order under s. 423.

s. 424(1)(a)

s. 424(2)

s. 425

The general duties of the court when asked to make an order are to restore the parties to the position in which they would have been if the transaction caught under s. 423 had not been entered into and to protect the persons on whose behalf the application is treated as having been made.

12.6.4 Extortionate credit transactions

A trustee can apply under the Act for an order in respect of an extortionate credit transaction, i.e., one in which, having regard to the risk accepted by the credit provider, the terms of the transaction required grossly exorbitant payments to be made (whether unconditionally or contingently) for the provision of credit, or otherwise grossly contravened the ordinary principles of fair dealing.

s. 343(2)

s. 343(3)

The transaction in respect of which the application is made is
s. 343(3) presumed to be extortionate unless the contrary is proved and the burden of proof, therefore, is on the credit provider.

The application can be made only in respect of transactions
s. 343(2) entered into within three years before the date of the bankruptcy order. However, a trustee in bankruptcy may be able, in appropriate circumstances, to attack an agreement as a transaction at an undervalue, under which sections he can look at transactions up to five years old. It is quite possible that grossly exorbitant or grossly unfair terms may involve an undervalue having regard to the definitions of 'significant' disparity in value given and received.

Anything recovered forms part of the bankrupt's estate. The court
s. 343(4) can set aside all or any obligations under the agreement, rewrite the bargain or any terms as to security, and order payments to be made or security to be surrendered.

12.6.5 Avoidance of general assignments of book debts

The 1914 Act in the marginal note to s. 43 referred to avoidance of 'general' assignments of book debts but did not use the word
s. 344 'general' in the text of that Act. The Act uses 'general' in the text. It also rearranges the 1914 Act provisions in a more logical fashion, but, except in relation to the time at which assigned debts must be paid to escape avoidance, it substantially reproduces the 1914 Act.

A 'general assignment' by a person engaged in business (the word 'trade' in the 1914 Act is omitted) of his existing or future book debts (or a class thereof) shall be void against the trustee in bankruptcy unless:

(a) the debts assigned were paid before the bankruptcy petition was presented; or

(b) the general assignment was registered under the Bills of Sale Act 1878 as though it were not an assignment by way of security under rules modifying the 1878 Act; or

(c) the assignment relates to debts becoming due under specified contracts; or

(d) the assignment is of book debts due at the date of assignment from specified debtors; or

(e) the assignment forms part of a transfer of a business, in good faith and for value; or

(f) the assignment is in an assignment of assets for the benefit of creditors generally.

12.6.6 Bankruptcy and enforcement procedures

The general aim of the Act is similar to that of the 1914 Act, with a few essential alterations in keeping with the new procedures leading up to a bankruptcy order.

Where a creditor issues execution against goods or land of the debtor, or attaches a debt due to the debtor, he is not entitled to retain the benefit of the execution or the attachment, or any sums paid to avoid it, unless the execution or attachment was complete, or the sums paid to avoid it were paid, before the commencement of bankruptcy. An execution against goods is completed by seizure and sale, or the making of a charging order under s. 1 of the Charging Orders Act 1979; an execution against land is completed by seizure, the appointment of a receiver, or a charging order being made; and an attachment of debt is completed by receipt of the debt. The reference to 'sums paid to avoid' a seizure and sale in s. 346(1) incorporates the effect of the decisions of the court in *Re Godwin* [1935] Ch 213, *Re Andrew* [1937] Ch 122 and *Marley Tile Co. Ltd* v *Burrows* [1978] QB 241 (CA). The commencement of bankruptcy is the making of the bankruptcy order, whereas under the 1914 Act bankruptcy commenced with the appropriate act of bankruptcy. s. 346(1) s. 278(a)

Where goods have been taken in execution and, before the execution is complete the sheriff is notified of a bankruptcy order, he must on request deliver to the official receiver or trustee in bankruptcy the goods and money seized or recovered in part satisfaction of the execution (subject to retention of his costs as a first charge on the subject-matter of the execution). Sums paid to avoid a seizure and sale are not 'in part satisfaction of the execution' and may therefore be claimed by the judgment creditor. *Marley Tile Co. Ltd* v *Burrows* [1978] QB 241 remains good law under the new Act. s. 346(2)

Where a sheriff levies execution under a judgment for a sum in excess of £500, and goods are sold or money is paid to avoid a sale, the sheriff must keep the balance for 14 days, and, if during that time he is notified of a petition upon which a bankruptcy order is made, he must not dispose of the balance until either the 14 days have expired or (if later) for so long as the petition of which he was notified is pending. If a bankruptcy order is made on that petition, the balance (subject to retention of his costs as a first charge) must be paid to the official receiver or trustee in bankruptcy. s. 346(3) and (4) SI 1986 No. 1996

A person who acquires, in good faith, any goods under a sale by the sheriff (or his officer charged with the execution) shall be safe from any claim by the trustee in bankruptcy. s. 346(7)

The court has a discretion to set aside any rights given to the trustee or official receiver under s. 346.

12.6.7 Landlords and distress

A landlord or other person to whom rent is payable has a right to levy

distress for six months' rent accrued due before bankruptcy
s. 347(9) commences. In so far as the right is lawfully exercisable, it can be exercised even though the estate has vested in the trustee in bankruptcy, but this right is subject to two important limitations:

s. 347(2) (a) Where the distress is against a lessee to whom a bankruptcy petition relates and a bankruptcy order is made thereon, the distress is effective only for rent payable during the six months prior to the bankruptcy order and if the distress is for a period after the time of distress it shall not be effective. In either case any sums recovered by an ineffective distress shall be held for the bankrupt as part of his estate.

(b) If there are insufficient assets to pay preferential creditors in full, the landlord or other persons to whom rent is payable must
s. 347(3) surrender goods or money taken under the distress to the trustee in bankruptcy. In this case the person so surrendering will rank as a preferential creditor but he cannot compete with the other preferential creditors for the assets he has surrendered.

s. 347(6) Where a landlord is entitled to claim for a year's rent under s. 1 of the Landlord and Tenant Act 1709 or s. 102 of the County Courts Act 1984 and the tenant is adjudged bankrupt before notice of the landlord's claim is served on the sheriff or officer charged with the execution, the landlord is limited to a claim for up to six months' rent
s. 347(7) and cannot distrain for rent due in respect of any period after the time of service of notice upon the sheriff or officer. A sheriff or officer who accounts to the landlord before being notified of the bankruptcy order is under no liability to the official receiver or trustee in bankruptcy. The landlord himself is not so protected.

There is nothing in s. 347 to prevent a landlord from proving in the
s. 347(10) bankruptcy for a debt in respect of rent.

12.7 Family homes

The Matrimonial Homes Act 1983 grants to a spouse who is not a legal owner of the matrimonial home rights of occupation which may be registered as a charge on the home and cannot be upset without a
s. 336(2) court order. The Act adapts these provisions to charge a spouse's right of occupation on the interest of the trustee in bankruptcy in the matrimonial home.

Where an application is made to realise the bankrupt's interest in the home, the court will have regard to the following factors:

(a) the interests of the creditors;

(b) whether or not the spouse's (or former spouse's) conduct has contributed to the bankruptcy; s. 336(4)
(c) the needs and resources of the spouse;
(d) the needs of any children;
(e) all relevant circumstances (other than the bankrupt's needs).

If the application is made after a year has elapsed since the bankrupt's property vested in the trustee in bankruptcy the creditors' interests shall be paramount. s. 336(5)

12.7.1 Jointly owned matrimonial homes

Where a bankrupt and his spouse (or former spouse) jointly own the matrimonial home, any application by the trustee in bankruptcy under the Law of Property Act 1925, s. 30, must be made to the bankruptcy court and is subject to the same discretionary factors listed above. s. 336(3)

12.7.2 Home in which children are living

Where a bankrupt has a beneficial interest or estate in a dwelling-house and has children under 18 years of age living there (both at the time of presentation of the petition and of the bankruptcy order), the bankrupt cannot be evicted without a court order (and with a court order he may reoccupy the dwelling if not in occupation at the time). The bankrupt's rights are a charge on his trustee's share in the dwelling, and the court's powers are discretionary. The court shall make such order as it thinks 'just and reasonable' having regard to: s. 337 s. 337(5)

(a) the creditors' interests;
(b) the bankrupt's financial resources;
(c) the needs of the children;
(d) all circumstances of the case other than the bankrupt's needs.

Chapter 13

Distribution of the Estate

13.1 Proof of claims

s. 322 The manner in which debts are to be proved, and the trustee's power to accept or reject proofs, are provided for in detail in the Rules. Any debt of uncertainty must be valued by the trustee (subject to appeal to the court under s. 303) and he must admit the proof at his (or the court's) valuation.

r. 12.3 All claims by creditors are provable as debts against the bankrupt whether these claims are present or future, certain or contingent, ascertained or sounding only in damages. The only debts that are not provable are:

(a) Any fine imposed for an offence (this implements the Cork Committee's recommendations and reverses *Re Pascoe* [1944] Ch 310).

(b) Any obligation arising under an order made in family or domestic proceedings.

(c) Any obligation arising under a confiscation order made under the Drug Trafficking Offences Act 1986, s. 1.

(d) Debts stated not to be provable in any other enactment or rule of law.

r. 6.93(2)
r. 6.96 Subject to dispensation by the court, any person wishing to recover his debt in whole or in part from the estate must submit a claim in writing to the trustee, or to the official receiver where he is acting as receiver and manager. The creditor must bear all the costs
r. 6.100 of proving. The proof must be in the prescribed, or a substantially
r. 6.96 similar, form unless the creditor is a Minister of the Crown or a Government Department. The form must be signed by or on behalf of the creditor and must state the creditor's name and address (or the
r. 6.98 name and address of the person signing on his behalf); the total claimed as at the date of the bankruptcy order and a statement as to whether or not this amount includes outstanding uncapitalised

interest or VAT; whether the debt or part of it is preferential; details of how and when the debt was incurred by the debtor; particulars of any security held by the creditor, including the date on which it was given and the creditor's valuation of it; and details of any documents by reference to which the claim may be substantiated. Unless the trustee or convener or chairman of any meeting requires otherwise, however, it is not necessary for the creditor to submit these documents with his proof. The trustee may require a claim to be verified by affidavit notwithstanding the fact that a proof of debt has r. 6.99 already been lodged. Proofs in respect of money owed on a bill of exchange etc., however, will be admitted only if accompanied by the r. 6.108 instrument itself or a copy thereof.

Every creditor who is known to the official receiver or trustee, or r. 6.97 who is identified in the bankrupt's statement of affairs, must be sent the necessary form on which to prove his debt. Subject to contrary ruling by the court, the form must be sent to the creditors at the same time as the earliest of the following notices:

(a) notice to creditors of the official receiver's decision not to call s. 293(2) a meeting of the creditors;
(b) first notice calling a meeting of creditors;
(c) notice sent by the official receiver where a certificate of summary administration has been issued by the court;
(d) notice to creditors of his appointment sent by a trustee appointed by the court unless, with leave of the court, he advertises his appointment, in which case proofs must be sent to creditors within four months after the date of the bankruptcy order.

When he is appointed, the trustee must have all proofs transmitted r. 6.103 to him by the official receiver and at all reasonable times on any r. 6.101 business day, the trustee must allow them to be inspected by the bankrupt, the proving creditors and their representatives.

A proof may at any time be withdrawn or varied by the creditor r. 6.106 with the consent of the trustee, and it may be expunged or varied by the court if the trustee shows that the proof was improperly admitted r. 6.107 or ought to be reduced or if the creditor appeals to the court following the trustee's refusal to allow a variation.

The trustee may admit a proof for dividend either in whole or in r. 6.104 part. If he decides to reject a proof or only to admit part of it he must send the creditor a written statement of his reasons. The creditor then r. 6.105 has 21 days from receipt of this statement to apply to the court to have the trustee's decision reversed or varied. A right of appeal to the court against the trustee's decision to admit or reject the whole or any part of a proof is also available to the bankrupt and to any other creditor. The application to the court must be made within 21 days of the bankrupt or creditor becoming aware of the trustee's decision.

13.2 Repeated bankruptcies

s. 335 Creditors in an earlier bankruptcy cannot prove in a later bankruptcy. The trustee in the earlier bankruptcy can, however, prove for any unsatisfied balance of debts (with interest) and expenses as a first charge on the assets in the later bankruptcy.

13.3 Quantification of claims

r. 6.110 For the purposes of quantifying a claim, all trade and other discounts
(other than discounts for immediate, early or cash settlements) must
r. 6.111 be deducted and, if the debt is incurred or payable other than in
sterling, the official exchange rate on the date of the bankruptcy
order, will prevail to convert the amount into sterling. The official
exchange rate is the middle market rate at the Bank of England on
the date in question. If there is no such rate, the court will decide
r. 6.112 the rate of exchange that is to apply. In the case of periodic payments,
such as rents, the creditor may prove for amounts due and unpaid up
to the date of the bankruptcy order.

r. 6.113 Even though it had not previously been reserved or agreed, interest may be claimed on the debt up to the date of the bankruptcy order but only if the debt was due by written instrument or, in other cases, if a written demand for payment had been made before presentation of the bankruptcy petition and notice had thereby been given that interest would be payable from that date until payment had been made. The rate of interest is that specified in Judgments Act 1838, s.17, or the amount specified in the written demand (if lower).

The fact that a debt was not due at the date of the bankruptcy
order does not prevent the creditor proving, but where payment is
not due when a dividend is declared, the debt will be reduced. The
r. 11.13 debt must, however, be satisfied in full before other creditors are
entitled to interest out of surplus funds under s. 328(4) (see 13.10).

13.4 Secured claims

r. 6.109 A secured creditor who realises his security may deduct the amount
realised and prove for the balance of the debt. If, on the other hand,
he voluntarily surrenders the security, he may prove for the whole
r. 6.116 debt as if it were unsecured. If he fails to disclose the security in his
proof of debt, however, he will be compelled to surrender it unless

such failure, in the court's opinion, was inadvertent or was the result of an honest mistake.

The secured creditor must value the security for the purpose of proving but, with the consent of the trustee or the court, he may amend this valuation at any time. If, however, he is the petitioner and has put a value on his security in the petition or if he has already voted in respect of the unsecured balance of his debt he may revalue the security only with leave of the court. On giving 28 days' notice, the trustee may at any time inform the creditor that he intends to redeem the security at the creditor's own valuation. The creditor then has 21 days within which to make a revaluation (subject to the above restrictions). At any time before a revaluation which has been approved by the court, a trustee who is dissatisfied with the creditor's valuation may require the property comprised in the security to be offered for sale on such terms as may be agreed between the parties or as are required by the court. Should the creditor realise the security, whether or not at the instance of the trustee, the amount thus realised will be substituted for the value previously estimated by the creditor and will be treated for all purposes as an amended valuation made by him. At any time the secured creditor may, in writing, require the trustee to elect whether or not to redeem the security at the creditor's valuation. The trustee then has six months within which to make his decision.

r. 6.115

r. 6.117

r. 6.118

r. 6.119

13.5 Set-off

The Act gives a right of set-off where there are mutual debts, mutual credits or other mutual dealings between the bankrupt and a third party. However, a debt due to the third party from the bankrupt shall not be set off if at the time when the debt became due the third party knew that a bankruptcy petition was pending. The Act is mandatory in form and contracting out of the right of set-off will not be possible either by the bankrupt or the third party.

s. 323

13.6 Distribution procedure

The general principles relating to the duties of the trustee and the distribution of the estate are:

(a) The trustee must first deduct what he considers necessary to cover expenses.

s. 324

(b) He must make allowances for claims that for geographical reasons may take time to reach him; for debts arising from as yet undetermined claims; disputed proofs; and the first charge on the

s. 325

distributable sum in his hands that a late-proving creditor enjoys for the amount of dividends that the creditor failed to receive because of the lateness of his proof.

s. 325(1) (c) A late-proving creditor cannot disturb previously paid dividends;

s. 326 (d) The trustee may with the consent of the creditors' committee distribute property *in specie* if such property cannot readily or advantageously be sold.

s. 324 (e) The trustee must give notice to the creditors of his intention to declare a dividend and, when he has declared it, notice of the manner of its distribution.

(f) In a criminal bankruptcy the trustee must not distribute if an appeal is pending.

13.7 Expenses

r. 6.224 The expenses of the bankruptcy are payable prior to any distribution, in the following order:

(a) expenses properly chargeable or incurred by the official receiver or the trustee in preserving or realising assets, including those incurred in acquiring title to after-acquired property;

(b) any other expenses incurred by the official receiver or under his authority, including those incurred in carrying on the business of a debtor or bankrupt;

(c) (i) the fee payable for the performance by the official receiver of his general duties as official receiver;

(ii) any repayable deposit lodged by the petitioner under any such order as security for the fee mentioned in (c)(i) (except where the deposit is applied to the payment of the remuneration of an insolvency practitioner appointed under s. 273 (see 10.2.4);

(d) any other fees payable including those payable to the official receiver, and any remuneration payable to him under general regulations;

(e) the cost of any security provided by an interim receiver, trustee or special manager;

(f) the remuneration of any interim receiver;

(g) any deposit lodged on an application for the appointment of an interim receiver;

(h) the costs of the petitioner, and of any person appearing on the petition whose costs are allowed by the court;

(i) the remuneration of any special manager;

(j) any amount payable to a person employed or authorised to help the bankrupt prepare a proper statement of affairs or accounts;

(k) any allowance made by the court towards costs on an application for release from the obligation to submit a statement of affairs, or for an extension of time for submitting such a statement;

(l) any necessary disbursements by the trustee in the course of his administration (including any expenses incurred by members of the creditors' committee or their representatives and allowed by the trustee, but not including any payment of capital gains tax in circumstances referred to in (o) below);

(m) the remuneration of any person (including the bankrupt) who has been employed by the trustee;

(n) the remuneration of the trustee, up to any amount not exceeding that which is payable to the official receiver under general regulations;

(o) the amount of any capital gains tax arising on the realisation of any asset of the bankrupt;

(p) the balance, after payment of any sums due under (n) above, of any remuneration due to the trustee.

Expenses incurred in holding an examination where the examinee is unfit and application for it is made by the official receiver, rank in priority with those specified in (a) above.

13.8 Declaration and payment of dividends

Before declaring a dividend, the trustee must give notice of his intention to do so to all creditors who have not yet proved. These r. 11.2
creditors must be given at least 21 days in which to lodge their proofs and the trustee must state his intention to declare a dividend, whether interim or final, within four months of this last date for proving.
Every creditor's proof must be dealt with by the trustee within seven r. 11.3
days of the last date for proving. Claims lodged after the 21-day period has expired may be admitted at the trustee's discretion. r. 11.4
During the four-month period before a dividend is declared, application may be made to the court to have the trustee's decision as to the admission or rejection of any proofs varied. If such application is made, the trustee may postpone or cancel the dividend. It follows that no application may be made outside the four-month period. If r. 11.5
no application is made or pending as to his decisions, the trustee will, after the four-month period has expired, proceed to declare the dividend. If an application is outstanding, the dividend may be declared only with leave of the court and subject to such provision being made in respect of the proof in question as the court may direct.

Notice of the dividend must be given to all creditors who have r. 11.6

proved and must contain details of realisations, payments made by the trustee, amounts retained, the total amount to be distributed and the rate of dividend, and whether any further dividend is expected to be declared.

The notice may be given at the same time as the dividend is paid, and payment may be made by post or in any other way agreed with
r. 11.11 any creditor. The right to receive a dividend may be assigned. If, however, the payment is on a bill of exchange etc. the amount of the dividend must be endorsed on the bill or on a certified copy of it.

r. 11.8 Once a dividend has been paid, a creditor who increases the amount claimed in his proof must wait for the extra payment to be made out of any further dividend. His claim will take priority over other recipients of this further dividend but he cannot disturb any distribution already made. Any over-payment to a creditor must be
r. 11.9 returned to the trustee. The same provisions apply in the case of a secured creditor who revalues his security after a dividend has been declared and, as a result, either increases or reduces the amount of his unsecured claim. Should such a secured creditor contravene any
r. 11.10 provision of the Act or the Rules in relation to the valuation of securities the court may, on the application of the trustee, order that he be wholly or partly disqualified from participation in any dividend.

r. 11.12 All these rules apply, with necessary modifications, to distributions made in the bankruptcy to preferential creditors.

13.9 Final distribution

s. 330 When the trustee has realised as much property as possible without needlessly protracting the administration of the estate he must notify all creditors of a final dividend (or that there will not be one, if that is the case) and give a final date for the proving of claims. He may then ignore in the final dividend the claims of any creditors who have not yet proved, but he must ensure that he has taken account of all outstanding expenses of the administration when calculating the dividend.

s. 331 One such expense is the cost of calling and holding the final meeting of creditors (which is held only when the trustee in bankruptcy is not the official receiver), at which the creditors receive the trustee's report of his administration and consider whether he
s. 332 should have his release. The final meeting must not be held when part of the bankrupt's estate includes an interest in a dwelling-house occupied by the bankrupt or spouse or former spouse when the trustee has not been able to sell, unless the court imposes a charge on the dwelling-house for the benefit of the estate or the court has

refused to impose any charge or the Secretary of State certifies that an application for a charge on the dwelling-house would be inappropriate.

13.10 Priority of payment

The Act prescribes the ranking of claims. These are set out below on the basis that debts in one class are only payable if debts in the earlier classes have been paid in full.

13.10.1 Specially preferred creditors
Where an articled clerk or apprentice has paid a fee, the trustee may pay a sum in respect of the unexpired period of his training (as at the date of the bankruptcy order), in which case the sum is paid before all other claims. s. 348

13.10.2 Preferential creditors
Preferential claims as specified in the Act, are calculated with reference to the period ending with the 'relevant date'. This is generally the date of the making of the bankruptcy order. If, however, an interim receiver was appointed following the presentation of a petition, the 'relevant date' is the date of that receiver's first appointment. s. 387(6)

If there are insufficient funds to pay all preferential claims in full, they abate equally.

The categories of preferential creditors are as follows: sch. 6

(a) 12 months' deductions of PAYE prior to the relevant date;

(b) 12 months' deductions of payments in respect of sub-contractors in the construction industry prior to the relevant date;

(c) VAT claims up to six months before the relevant date;

(d) car tax, general betting duty, bingo duty, gaming licence duty, amounts of any agent's liability for general betting and pool betting duty in respect of collected stakes for 12 months before the relevant date;

(e) assessments of Class 1 or Class 2 national insurance contributions for 12 months prior to the relevant date;

(f) one year's assessment of Class 4 contributions before 5 April prior to the relevant date;

(g) State and occupational pension scheme contributions (see Social Security Pensions Act 1975, sch. 3);

(h) employees' arrears of wages or salary for four months prior to the relevant date subject to a limit of £800. This includes payments in respect of sick pay, protective awards, payments during medical suspension and time off work (e.g., on trade union work);

(i) accrued holiday remuneration;

(j) advances by a third party for the payment of emoluments or holiday remuneration that would, but for the payment, have fallen within (h) and (i) above;

(k) money ordered to be paid for defaults in the Reserve Forces (Safeguard of Employment) Act 1985, in respect of defaults occurring before the bankruptcy order was made;

s. 328 (l) any other debts declared preferential by any other enactment.

13.10.3 Ordinary creditors

s. 328 Ordinary creditors are those who are neither preferred nor postponed under the Act. If there are insufficient funds to pay them in full they abate equally. Contractual interest over 5% is no longer deferred as it was under the Bankruptcy Act 1914.

13.10.4 Statutory interest

s. 328 If a surplus remains after all previous claims are met, interest from the date of the bankruptcy order to the date of payment shall be paid next. The interest is to be the greater of:

(a) that applicable under the Judgments Act 1838, s. 17, (currently 15%); and

(b) the rate of interest that the bankrupt would have had to pay in respect of the debt if he had not been adjudicated bankrupt.

13.10.5 Transactions between spouses

s. 329 Where a person married to the bankrupt at the date of the bankruptcy order has a provable debt because of credit provided for the bankrupt, that debt ranks behind all other debts referred to so far. If this debt is paid then statutory interest as described in 13.10.4. is also payable.

13.10.6 Surplus

s. 330 Any surplus belongs to the bankrupt.

Chapter 14

Duration of Bankruptcy and Discharge

14.1 Introduction

Under the Bankruptcy Act 1914 a bankruptcy commenced with the first act of bankruptcy committed within three months before the presentation of the petition. The policy behind this enactment was that the commission of an act of bankruptcy evidenced insolvency and if at that time a person could not pay his creditors in full he should pay them rateably out of his assets.

The new Act, on the other hand, has jettisoned entirely the concept of acts of bankruptcy and the policy which gave rise to it has been modified as well. Bankruptcy now commences with the day upon which the bankruptcy order is made. One consequence of this is that the old doctrine of relation back of the trustee's title, under which assets retrospectively vested in the trustee, has ceased to be of relevance.

Bankruptcy continues until the bankrupt is discharged. Again, the thinking has changed with regard to discharge. Under the Bankruptcy Act 1914, discharge was a matter for the court's discretion and an application for discharge was subject to a wide range of factors which affected that discretion. In particular, on proof of any of the so-called 'facts' (such as undue preference, assets not equal to 50p in the pound, frivolous litigation on the bankrupt's part), the bankrupt could not obtain an immediate absolute discharge. In the Insolvency Act 1976, however, the concept of automatic discharge by effluxion of time was introduced, though the courts remained firmly committed to their discretionary powers under the Bankruptcy Act 1914 and overlaid the 'automatic' approach of the 1976 Act with the old discretions (see *Re Reed* [1980] Ch 212).

The Government, as it promised in its White Paper, *A Revised Framework for Insolvency Law* (Cmnd 9175), has travelled further down the road to automatic discharge by lapse of time and the Act has removed the old discretions from the statute book. It may be, however, that the Act is not nearly as 'automatic' in its approach as was perhaps envisaged, since it contains a provision to the effect that the running of time leading to automatic discharge by lapse may be stopped by the court if the bankrupt has failed to carry out any of his obligations under the Act. The court is arguably given a greater discretion than before to refuse absolute discharge, since the scope of the bankrupt's obligations under the Act is much wider than anything in the Bankruptcy Act 1914 and the Insolvency Act 1976.

14.2 Duration of bankruptcy

s. 278 The general rule is that bankruptcy commences with the day upon which the bankruptcy order is made and continues until such time as the bankrupt obtains his discharge.

The time that the bankrupt obtains his discharge is as follows:

s. 279(2)(a) (a) Summary administrations: two years from the making of the bankruptcy order.

ss. 279 and 280 (b) Criminal or repeated bankruptcy: where a criminal bankruptcy order was made, or where the debtor had been an undischarged bankrupt at any time in 15 years prior to the present bankruptcy, discharge is obtainable only by means of a court order, for which application may be made when five years have elapsed since the bankruptcy order was made. In making his application,
r. 6.217 the bankrupt must give notice to the official receiver and deposit with him such sum as the latter may require to cover the costs of the application. The court must give the official receiver and the bankrupt at least 42 days' notice of the hearing of the application and, at least 14 days before the date fixed for the hearing, the official receiver must give notice of it to the trustee and to any creditor with a
r. 6.218 claim outstanding against the estate. Also, at least 21 days before the date of the hearing, the official receiver must file in court a report on the bankrupt detailing:

(i) any failure by the bankrupt to comply with his obligations under the Act;

(ii) the circumstances surrounding the present bankruptcy and any previous bankruptcies;

(iii) the extent to which, in the present and any previous bankruptcy, his liabilities have exceeded his assets;

(iv) particulars of any distribution made or expected to be made to creditors in the present bankruptcy or the fact that no distribution has been made or is expected;

(v) any other matters the official receiver considers necessary to be brought to the court's attention.

Copies of the report must be sent by the official receiver to both the trustee and the bankrupt to reach them not less than 14 days before the hearing. The bankrupt must, at least seven days before the hearing, file in court a notice specifying any statements in the report which he intends to deny or dispute. Copies of this notice by the bankrupt must be sent by him to the official receiver and the trustee not less than four days before the hearing.

At the hearing, the official receiver, trustee and any creditor may appear and make representations and put such questions to the bankrupt as the court may allow. At the hearing the court may allow, s. 280 refuse or suspend the discharge and/or make it conditional upon future income or property, although the order will not be issued or r. 6.221 gazetted until the time allowed for an appeal has expired or, if an appeal is made, until the appeal has been determined. An order for the absolute or conditional discharge of the bankrupt will take effect r. 6.219 from the time it is drawn up by the court but will relate back to the date the actual order was made. Copies of this order must be sent by the court to the bankrupt, the trustee and the official receiver.

(c) Other cases (this will be the majority of cases): automatically s. 279(2)(b) after three years have elapsed since the bankruptcy order was made. The automatic right can be defeated if the official receiver satisfies s. 279(3) the court that there is or has been a failure on the part of the bankrupt to comply with any of his obligations under the Act. To apply for an r. 6.215 order suspending the automatic discharge, the official receiver must file a report in support of his application, and send a copy of it to the trustee and the bankrupt. This copy must be received at least 21 days before the date fixed by the court for the hearing. If the bankrupt wishes to dispute or deny any parts of the report he must file in court a notice specifying these matters at least seven days before the date of the hearing and copies of the notice must be sent by him to the official receiver and trustee at least four days before the hearing.

At the hearing, the court may simply order that time under the three-year period shall stop running. It must send copies of this order to the bankrupt, the official receiver and the trustee. The court has wide discretion and automatic discharge may not be as automatic as might appear to be the case at first sight.

The bankrupt against whom an order suspending automatic r. 6.216 discharge has been made may apply to the court for the order to be removed. The court will fix a time and place for the hearing and, at least 28 days before the application is due to be heard, the bankrupt must give notice of it, together with a copy of his application, to the official receiver and the trustee, both of whom have a right to be heard. The official receiver, whether he appears or not, has the right to file a report detailing information which he considers ought to be brought to the court's attention, including a statement as to whether any conditions imposed by the court have been fulfilled. Copies of this report must be sent by the official receiver to the bankrupt and the trustee at least 14 days before the hearing and, no later than seven days before the hearing, the bankrupt may file in court a notice specifying any matters in the report which he disputes or denies. He must send copies of this notice to the official receiver and the trustee at least four days before the date of the hearing. If the court decides to grant the bankrupt's application and remove the suspension of his discharge, it will issue the bankrupt with a certificate stating this and giving effect to the removal from a specified date.

14.2.1 Certificate of discharge

r. 6.220 When a bankrupt is discharged the court will issue to him a certificate of discharge whether this discharge has come about by expiration of time or otherwise. The date of discharge will be specified in the certificate. The discharged bankrupt may require the Secretary of State to give notice of the discharge in the *Gazette* and/or any newspaper in which the bankruptcy was advertised. The cost of so advertising must be borne by the applicant and will be payable in advance. These rights are available to the personal representative of a deceased former bankrupt and to the person appointed to represent or act for a former bankrupt who is incapable of managing
r. 7.43 his own affairs by reason of mental disorder within the meaning of the Mental Health Act 1983 or due to physical affliction or disability.

r. 6.222 In no case will any costs or expenses involved in the discharge of the bankrupt or in any proceedings related to the discharge fall on the official receiver personally.

14.3 Effect of discharge

s. 281 Generally, discharge releases the bankrupt from his bankruptcy debts. However, a number of obligations and liabilities may remain:

(a) where the trustee in bankruptcy still has functions to perform, the Act remains in full force to enable the functions to be carried out;

(b) creditors may still prove their debts (though dividends paid cannot be disturbed);

(c) secured creditors may still realise their security;

(d) the bankrupt still remains liable in respect of non-provable debts;

(e) liability for the following provable debts still continues:

(i) where the liability is for fraud or fraudulent breach of trust;

(ii) fines and recognisances;

(iii) liability for personal injuries arising from negligence, nuisance, breach of contract, breach of statutory duty or any other duty, or arising under any order made in family proceedings or domestic proceedings, unless the court orders otherwise;

(f) the bankrupt is not released from obligations arising under a confiscation order made under the Drug Trafficking Offences Act 1986, s. 1. r. 6.223

14.4 Annulment of bankruptcy order

The court may annul a bankruptcy order in the following circumstances:

(a) if it should not have been made; s. 282

(b) if the bankruptcy debts and expenses have all been paid or secured since the making of the order;

(c) if a proposed voluntary arrangement by an undischarged bankrupt is approved by his creditors. s. 261

Chapter 15

Winding-up Insolvent Partnerships

15.1 Introduction

The law governing the winding-up of insolvent partnerships is set out in the Insolvent Partnerships Order 1986 (the 'Order'). This Order, which applies in England and Wales, specifies the provisions of the Act which apply in relation to insolvent partnerships and the modifications to certain of those provisions. The Order applies only where an insolvent partnership is being wound up and does not affect the winding-up of corporate partners and the bankruptcy of individual partners in other cases, which can take place under the Act in the normal manner. The Order also applies certain provisions of the Company Directors Disqualification Act 1986.

15.2 Provisions as to winding-up

The following summary of the provisions is drawn from the explanatory notes to the Order:

(a) An insolvent partnership may be wound up under Part V of the Act (winding-up of unregistered companies) as an unregistered company without involving the insolvency of the partners. The provisions of Part V that apply with relevant modifications are specified in sch. 1 to the Order. These include s. 221, subsection (1) of which applies all the provisions of the Act and the Companies Act 1985 about winding-up with exceptions and additions, and subsection (4) of which provides that the partnership can only be wound up by the court (art. 7).

(b) An insolvent partnership may be wound up under Part V of the Act as an unregistered company involving the insolvency of two or more partners. Sections 220(1) and 221 are applied with modifications and, as above, this involves the application of all the provisions of the Act and the Companies Act 1985 about winding-up by the court with exceptions and additions and with the modifications in pt I of sch. 2 to the Order (art. 8(1)).

(c) The Order also provides for the winding-up of corporate partners and the bankruptcy of individual partners of an insolvent partnership in conjunction with the winding-up of the partnership as an unregistered company under Part V of the Act. The provisions of the Act about winding-up by the court and bankruptcy apply, with the modifications specified in pts II and III of sch. 2 to the Order respectively (art. 8(2)). Petitions cannot be presented under Part IX of the Act (bankruptcy) against the partnership or against the individual partners in the name of the firm (sch. 2, pt III, para. 1). There are provisions about priority of expenses and debts (arts 9 and 10).

(d) The provisions of Parts I and VIII of the Act dealing with voluntary arrangements are applied in relation to corporate and individual members of an insolvent partnership respectively, if the proposal made for a composition or scheme of arrangement includes all the creditors of the partnership (art. 11).

(e) The Order also makes provisions in respect of insolvency proceedings against members of an insolvent partnership not involving the winding-up of the partnership as an unregistered company (arts 13 and 14).

(f) Where an insolvent partnership is being wound up under Part V of the Act as an unregistered company, any member or former member of the partnership or any other person who has or has had control or management of the partnership business:

(i) shall for the purposes of the provisions of the Act and the Company Directors Disqualification Act 1986 applied by the Order be deemed to be an officer and director of the company; and

(ii) shall deliver up to the liquidator of the partnership for the purposes of the exercise of the liquidator's functions under the provisions referred to in paragraph (i) above possession of any partnership property within the meaning of the Partnership Act 1890 which he holds for the purposes of the partnership.

(g) Where an insolvent partnership is wound up as an unregistered company under Part V of the Act certain provisions of the Company Directors Disqualification Act 1986 apply in relation to the partnership as if any member of the partnership were a director of a company, and the partnership were a company as defined by that Act as one that may be wound up under Part V of the Act. The provisions are:

(i) s. 6 (duty of court to disqualify unfit directors of insolvent companies);

(ii) s. 7 (applications to court under s. 6, and reporting provisions);

(iii) s. 8 (disqualification after investigation of company);

(iv) s. 9 (matters for determining unfitness of director);

(v) s. 10 (participation in wrongful trading);

(vi) s. 15 (personal liability for company's debts where person acts while disqualified);

(vii) s. 19(c) (provision precluding application under ss. 6 or 8 where company went into liquidation before 28 April 1986);

(viii) s. 20 (admissibility in evidence of statements);

(ix) sch. 1 (details of matters for determining unfitness of directors).

Chapter 16

Bankruptcy Offences

16.1 Introduction

Although bankruptcy is not a criminal offence, the old attitude to acts of bankruptcy was that they were a species of fraud, so that bankruptcy has always hovered around the edge of the criminal law (see Blackstone's *Commentaries*, bk. 2, ch. 31). Penalties imposed on the bankrupt were severe. Blackstone pointed out in the middle of the 18th century that the offences of concealment of assets with intent to defraud creditors, and of failure to deliver up writings and records pertaining to the bankrupt's business, both carried the death penalty (Blackstone's *Commentaries*, bk. 4, 1st ed., p. 156).

The Bankruptcy Act 1914 contained a mixture of offences that might have been simplified but, because the older statutory expressions have acquired established meanings and because the process of simplification is not complete, these offences have been retained with some modifications.

The offences will be considered under four headings:

16.2 Improper dealings in property
16.3 Failure to deliver up property
16.4 Failure to make proper disclosure of conduct, dealings, affairs and property
16.5 Misleading creditors

This does not follow the order in which the offences appear in the Act but it may make it easier to understand the aims of the criminal law in this area.

16.2 Improper dealings in property

(a) If a bankrupt makes, causes to be made, or, within five years before the bankruptcy order has made (or caused) any gift, transfer or charge on his property or has caused, or connived at the levying of execution upon his property, he commits an offence. s. 357(1) s. 357(2)

This offence, like many listed below, is strict in form. The prosecution's burden of proof ends at the point above; in particular, therefore, the prosecution does not have the burden of proving fraud

s. 352 — indeed fraud is not referred to. However, fraud is the substance of the offence because the Act provides that the bankrupt can escape liability if he proves that he had no intent to defraud his creditors or to conceal the state of his affairs at the time of the transaction. The burden of proving innocence is upon the bankrupt, so that if the bankrupt tenders no evidence, or the evidence which he gives is equivocal or those charged with deciding guilt or innocence are not sure, the bankrupt must be convicted.

s. 357(3) (b) If a bankrupt has concealed or removed any of his property within two months before, or any time after, a money judgment was unsatisfied, he commits an offence.

There is no time-limit set upon the period before the making of a bankruptcy order during which the bankrupt's action can be investi-

s. 352 gated. As with the offence in (a) above, the bankrupt is to be acquitted if he proves no intent to defraud or to conceal the state of his affairs.

s. 358 (c) Where, after a bankruptcy order is made, the bankrupt leaves (or attempts or prepares to leave) England and Wales with property (with a minimum value of at least £500) that he ought to hand over to his trustee in bankruptcy or the official receiver, he is guilty of an offence unless he proves that he had no intention to defraud creditors or conceal the state of his affairs.

All property which forms or would have formed part of the estate (including after-acquired property or property subject to a s. 308 notice) is included in this section. The section also extends to departures (or attempted departures) that occur between the petition and the bankruptcy order, and to those occurring up to six months before the petition was presented (subject of course, to the same defence).

s. 354(2) (d) Unless he proves no intent to defraud or conceal the state of
and s. 352 his affairs, a bankrupt is liable to conviction if he removes, after presentation of a petition, any property above the value of £500 which would or should form part of his estate.

s. 359(1) (e) If at any time between 12 months before the presentation of a
and (5) petition and the making of the bankruptcy order, the bankrupt disposes of, pawns or pledges property bought on credit and not paid for, he commits an offence.

The bankrupt has a good defence if he can show either that he had no intention to defraud creditors or that he did not intend to conceal

s. 359(3) the state of his affairs, and that the transaction amounting to a
and (4) disposal took place in the 'ordinary course of business'. In assessing

whether a transaction is in the ordinary course of business the Act makes the price at which the property was sold a relevant consideration. Therefore sales at greatly reduced prices may well be equivalent to fraud.

(f) An offence is committed if an undischarged bankrupt fails to disclose his status to all persons concerned whenever he enters (alone or jointly) into any of the following transactions: s. 360

(i) Obtaining credit. (This was an offence under the Bankruptcy Act 1914.) s. 360(1)(a)

(ii) Entering into a hire-purchase transaction. This provision is new and reverses the effect of *R* v *Miller* [1977] 1 WLR 1129 in which it was held that entering into a hire-purchase agreement did not involve obtaining credit.

(iii) Entering into a conditional sale agreement. s. 360(2)(a)

(iv) Accepting payment in advance for the supply of goods and services. s. 360(2)(b)

(v) Engaging directly or indirectly in business in a name other than the name stated in his bankruptcy order. s. 360(1)(b)

It should be noted here that the defence that the bankrupt has no intent to defraud creditors, which applies to many of the offences referred to above, is not available.

(g) A bankrupt commits an offence if, during the two years before the presentation of the petition, it appears that he has 'materially' contributed to or increased the extent of his insolvency by gambling, or entering into rash or hazardous speculations. Whether a speculation is rash or hazardous obviously turns on the nature of the speculation, but that is not the only factor. The Act directs that the financial position of the bankrupt is a circumstance to be weighed when assessing the rashness or hazard involved. s. 362(1)(a) s. 362(2)

It may be presumed that a once-a-year 'flutter' of 50p on the Grand National is not 'material' for these purposes.

(h) Section 362 takes gambling and improper speculation a little further. If a bankrupt has pursued such activities between the date of the presentation of the petition and the bankruptcy order and in so doing has lost any part of his property he is guilty of an offence. The Act no longer requires that the loss be 'material' as a precondition of liability.

(i) Section 359 imposes criminal liability on a person who acquires property from a bankrupt during the period from 12 months before the presentation of a petition to the bankruptcy order where that person knows or believes that the bankrupt has not paid for it and that the bankrupt did not intend or was unable to pay for the property.

16.3 Failure to deliver up property

s. 354(1)(a) (a) Where a bankrupt has in his possession or control any property which he is under a legal obligation to deliver up, he must deliver to, or as directed by, the official receiver or the trustee in bankruptcy, otherwise an offence is committed.

s. 354(1)(b) SI 1986 No. 1996 (b) Where a bankrupt conceals property, if the value of the property exceeds £500, or conceals any debts due to him, he commits an offence.

s. 354(1)(c) (c) A bankrupt may similarly be made liable where he has concealed property at any time during 12 months before presentation of the petition and the bankruptcy order.

In these three cases the bankrupt will have a defence if he proves that he had no intent to defraud creditors or conceal the state of his affairs.

16.4 Failure to make proper disclosure of conduct, dealings, affairs and property

s. 353(1)(a) (a) It is an offence for a bankrupt to fail to disclose to the official receiver or the trustee in bankruptcy all property comprised in his estate to the best of his knowledge and belief, unless he shows that he had no intent to defraud or to conceal the state of his affairs.

s. 354(1)(b) (b) A bankrupt may be made criminally liable if he conceals any debts due to or from him. A defence of no intent to defraud creditors or conceal the state of his affairs is available to the bankrupt.

s. 353(2) (c) Except for disposals of property in the ordinary course of business, a bankrupt may be convicted of an offence if he has failed
s. 353(1)(a) to inform the official receiver or the trustee in bankruptcy of property that, if not disposed of, would have formed part of his
s. 353(1)(b) estate. The obligation extends to giving details of how, when and to whom it was disposed and any consideration received. The defence of no intent to defraud or conceal the state of the bankrupt's affairs is available.

s. 354(3) (d) A bankrupt may be made criminally liable if, without reasonable excuse, he fails to account for, or satisfactorily explain, the manner or the loss of a substantial part of his property occurring during the period from 12 months before the presentation of a petition to the making of the bankruptcy order.

s. 356(2)(b) (e) It is a crime for a bankrupt to attempt to account for any part of his property by fictitious losses or expenses.

s. 355(2)(b) (f) A bankrupt may be convicted if he conceals, mutilates, destroys or falsifies any book, paper or other record (or causes or permits such acts) at any of the following times:

(i) after the bankruptcy order; s. 355(2)(d)

(ii) between presentation of the petition and the making of the bankruptcy order;

(iii) during 12 months before the petition was presented;

(iv) in relation to proper accounting records, during two years before presentation of the petition. s. 361(4)

(g) If, at any of the times specified in paragraph (f), a bankrupt makes false entries in books, documents or records relating to his estate or affairs, he may be convicted of an offence unless he shows that he had no intent either to defraud creditors or to conceal the state of his affairs. s. 355(2)(c)

(h) Similarly, at the same time and subject to the same defences as set out in paragraph (g), a bankrupt is guilty of an offence if he disposes of, alters or makes any omission in any book, document or record, relating to his estate or affairs. s. 355(3)(a)

(i) To make a material omission in a statement of affairs is an offence unless the bankrupt proves no intent either to defraud or to conceal the state of his affairs. s. 356(1)

(j) A bankrupt is liable to criminal penalty if, as soon as is practicable after he knows or believes a false debt to have been proved, he does not notify the trustee in bankruptcy. s. 356(2)

(k) Whilst generally failing to keep proper records of business activities is not in itself a criminal act, it can become one where bankruptcy ensues. The lower limit of a bankrupt's unsecured liabilities is £20,000 and any bankrupt whose unsecured liabilities exceed that limit, and who has engaged in business between two years before the petition was presented and the date of the bankruptcy order, is guilty of an offence if he has not kept and preserved 'proper' accounting records. Records will not be 'proper' unless they show or explain the bankrupt's transactions and financial position regarding: s. 361

(i) cash received and paid;

(ii) annual stocktakings (where appropriate);

(iii) except for retail sales, the identities of his sellers and buyers.

It will be a defence to show that the omission to keep such records was honest and excusable.

16.5 Misleading creditors

(a) If at any time between 12 months before the presentation of a petition and the making of the bankruptcy order, the bankrupt has s. 356(2)(b) and (c) misled a meeting of his creditors by attempting to account for property by raising fictitious losses or expenses, he becomes criminally liable.

s. 356(2)(d) (b) If at any time a bankrupt has made false representations, or committed any other kind of fraud to induce any creditor or creditors to enter into any agreement relating to his affairs or bankruptcy, he commits an offence.

Index